TO BE
DISPOSED
BY
AUTHORITY

THE
WAY WE LIVE
NOW

Bernard Levin

THE
WAY WE LIVE
NOW

JONATHAN CAPE
THIRTY BEDFORD SQUARE LONDON

First published 1984
Reprinted 1984
Copyright © 1984 by Bernard Levin

Jonathan Cape Ltd, 30 Bedford Square, London WC1B 3EL

British Library Cataloguing in Publication Data
Levin, Bernard
The way we live now.
1. Great Britain—Social life and customs—20th century
I. Title
082   DA592

ISBN 0–224–02272–5

Phototypeset by Falcon Graphic Art Ltd
Wallington, Surrey
Printed in Great Britain by
Butler & Tanner Ltd
Frome and London

Contents

Introduction

IN 1979 I PUT FORTH, under the title *Taking Sides* and the imprint of Jonathan Cape (publishers of all my books), a volume of my journalism, the items in which were selected, with only three exceptions, from my work in the decade then coming to an end. In 1982 I published a second such compilation, entitled *Speaking Up*; this covered the same period, and nothing in it dated from before 1972. These two volumes between them, I declared, contained all the journalism I wished to preserve from among the thousands of articles of all kinds I had written in the thirty or so years of my career; most of these I had not kept at all, and I then destroyed the remainder of what I had. Any subsequent book of my journalism, therefore, would begin where the previous one left off; I recall that I experienced a perhaps naive feeling of renewal and a fresh start. So *The Way We Live Now* consists only of articles published (in *The Times* or the *Observer*) from October 1982 onwards.*

*Once more I am indebted to my secretary, Sally Chichester, for all her indispensable and invaluable help. The index is again the work of Oula Jones, of the Society of Indexers, who has brought to what is always an exacting task, and too frequently a thankless one, all her skill, patience and good humour. The proofs were again read by Brian Inglis, whose all-seeing eye spotted many a mistake in time.

But behind the bare chronology lies something that is perhaps worth explaining.

In the introduction to *Speaking Up* I told of my discovery that I was suffering from chronic 'workaholism', a thrall no less powerful and potentially damaging than the more familiar addictions to drink or drugs, and disclosed that I had, faced with this ominous realisation, decided upon and abruptly taken very drastic action; in April 1981 I resigned simultaneously from both my positions in regular journalism (as columnist for *The Times* and fiction reviewer for the *Sunday Times*), 'determined', as I said, 'to follow the beckoning light wherever it might lead . . . and moreover without setting a term to my period at large'.

Flinging off his coat, at one bound Jack was free. But what then? The first shock was the greatest; I found that I suffered no withdrawal symptoms at all. In the vast sabbatical I had so blithely entered upon (it lasted, in the end, exactly eighteen months), I never once found myself, when, say, reading the newspapers at breakfast, yearning to get to my typewriter and comment upon the affairs of the world. I did continue to experience my normal feelings at the course of those affairs – interest, curiosity, amazement, rage, hilarity, disgust – but I felt not the smallest impulse to deliver myself of my views thereon: *Que l'humanité se débrouille sans moi.*

For a man who had made his living (and enjoyed doing so) by public comment for more than a quarter of a century, this was a startling discovery, causing me to wonder what mysterious bottle labelled Drink Me I must have been absent-mindedly swigging from. Detachment was almost the only response I had never felt in public matters; why was I now lapped in it?

I worked out the answer – or at any rate an answer – only slowly, just as I had earlier found it difficult to awaken to the painful truth behind my self-imposed slavery to a timetable so demanding that it left me no time to think about anything else. I had come to the conclusion that that bondage was designed, deliberately even though unconsciously, to prevent me from putting my work into proper perspective as a necessary and agreeable part of life but by no means the most important; now I had to face a further realisation, no less unwelcome at first than the earlier one, yet no less illuminating and valuable when faced.

It was not that I no longer cared about the great questions I had for so long dealt in – injustice, the totalitarian mind abroad and at home, politics and economics, the follies and misdemeanours of those set in authority over us ('Dost thou not know, my son, with how little wisdom the world is governed?'), the swings and roundabouts of outrageous fortune among our leaders, the truths of history and its more numerous falsehoods, the cultural developments that, at first hailed as of eternal significance, proved as easily disposable as cheap ball-point pens – these, as I say, continued to exercise their varying forms of fascination for me; the detachment I have described concerned only my wish to comment upon them. I was, to put it plainly, sick of the sound of my own voice: why? (Would reviewers of this volume kindly note that I have already thought of all the answers to that question they might feel inclined to give, and indeed I would have included them as an appendix if I had not decided that they were too obvious.)

It took a lot of thought and a lot of work before I could offer myself a tentative explanation; I have no intention of going into the kind of detail that would be appropriate in an autobiography, which I shall certainly never write, but since in my last book I went further than I had previously done in describing the events of my life, I shall be going no further in now discussing those inner conclusions that are surely at least as important as the external influences which shape our ends, rough-hew them how we may.

For a middle-aged man to begin to experience dissatisfaction with his life and work is not very surprising; indeed, there can be few who have never felt it. Nor has the phenomenon anything to do with the lack of achievement: 'they met me in the day of *success*,' says Macbeth. On the contrary, the more fruitful the career, the more settled the domestic life, the more ample the income, the sharper the gnawing, at any rate for those of any imagination at all, as they begin to suspect that ultimate reality lies elsewhere, glimpsed out of the corner of the eye, sensed just beyond the light cast by the camp-fire, heard in the slow movement of a Mozart quartet, seen in the eyes of Rembrandt's last self-portraits, felt in the sudden stab of discovery in reading or seeing a Shakespeare play thought familiar in every line.

Not long after I embarked on the unknown sea of my sabbatical, I was sitting on my sofa alone as dusk fell. I was not reading, listening to music or even thinking; I remember wondering idly whether to draw the curtains, and deciding not to, then giving myself up entirely to the silent serenity of the evening. After a time, perhaps half an hour, I realised how seldom, in the past twenty years and more, I had spent any time at all doing nothing. I searched the recesses of memory for such moments, and could find pitifully few, embedded like currants in a miser's cake, among the activity. I stayed where I was, but now thinking hard: why had I so filled my days and nights, why had I been so determined to leave no empty space in my life or my mind, what was it that I had feared so much that I had been willing to drive myself to exhaustion (in every sense of the word) in an attempt to keep it out?

The obvious answer is too obvious even to mention. But this Introduction is not an account of my own search, which I shall describe, if at all, in a book devoted entirely to it. All I want to do here is to trace the roots of my new-found attitude to the many millions of words I had committed to print and to the airwaves, an attitude which had led to the revulsion (the word is not too strong) I have described.

All journalists who live by comment are troubled from time to time by the thought that nobody is listening, and that nothing would happen even if somebody, or even everybody, were. This is a salutary, indeed an essential, feeling; we all know that to move with words alone a spadeful of earth, never mind a mountain, is practically impossible. (There was one television critic in Britain who was fond of demanding in print the dismissal of newsreaders and other broadcasters whom he disliked, and then expressing what I am sure was a perfectly genuine astonishment and anger when they remained in their posts. But that is a rather unusual attitude.) I have often been horrified by the tone of some of the letters I get from readers wishing to enlist me in some cause dear to them; the writers seem to think that I have only to pick up my pen for the wrong to be righted, the motorway diverted, the pension paid, the building left undemolished, the sinner brought to repentance, the righteous exalted. The unease such correspondents cause me is, no doubt, partly a realisation that I must, by the way I write, have given them reason to believe that I have a magic wand, an alchemist's touchstone and the instantly forthcoming co-operation of a wide variety of Prime Ministers, Archbishops and foreign potentates, whereas the best and most I can claim is a few unlisted telephone numbers and a vast collection of non-committal replies. (Mind you, the doorman at Fortnum & Mason once became so frustrated and self-reproachful at his inability to find me a taxi that he fetched his own car and drove me home. Could Walter Cronkite say as much?) But the disquiet is much more a product of my knowledge that very little ever changes at all, and that even less changes because I argue that it should, nor have I ever found much comfort in Balfour's parallel axiom: 'Not everything matters, and nothing matters very much.'

The crossroads of middle age commonly provide a gloomy view; the terrain ahead looks uncomfortably similar to that behind, except that it seems to slope inexorably downwards, and Housman's delicious self-pity (I have been reading him most of my life, in comfortable armchairs, with fascination and incredulity) suddenly seems serious:

> Now hollow fires burn out to black,
> And lamps are guttering low;
> Square your shoulders, lift your pack,
> And leave your friends and go.
>
> Nay, never fear, lad, nought's to dread,
> Look not left nor right;
> In all the endless road you tread,
> There's nothing but the night.

But life, however implacable, does not actually cheat; a cure for the gloom of middle age is to translate it into Italian. *Nel medio del cammin di nostra vita* serves to remind us of the fact that the work it begins was born of an earthly disappointment and was started when the poet was three-quarters of the way through his life. (It also serves to remind *me* that it was finished when he was exactly the same age as I am as I write these words, and that he died the following year. I am not sure that that adds anything to my own consolation, but I am trying to be helpful.)

It was in this curious mood that I found myself, day after day at breakfast, reading the news without the old impulse to do anything about it. Of course, the experience was not as abrupt or tidy as I have made it, for simplicity's sake, appear; there had been many occasions in the past when I had wondered whether spitting into the wind was really an occupation for grownups, and not merely because it so often led to nothing but an eyeful of spit. Nor, for that matter, was I seized, that first day without a column to write, with a searing realisation that my entire career had been a waste of time, followed by a feverish search for a hammer with which to smash my typewriter and a rope to fashion into a noose. But I did come fairly quickly to a conclusion and a decision. The conclusion was that, in the burden of work I had laid upon myself I must have been, in some real sense, almost literally deranged; the decision was that, whenever I returned to journalism, it would be to a weekly tally of words not more than a third of the previous score.

At that point I put from me all further thought of how and where and when I would arrange this happy consummation, content with the feeling that so striking a change could not but bring about some radical trans-formation of my life, and that meanwhile I would at any rate have more time and breathing-space in which to think about the view from those crossroads. To mark the spot, I embarked upon the work that ultimately led to my most recent book, *Enthusiasms*,* and I very speedily realised that it would be a book unlike anything I had written before. That in itself meant nothing; as it happens, my next book will be even more unlike anything I have written before, including *Enthusiasms*. But in trying to formulate and describe the essence of those experiences from which I have, throughout my life, derived joy and solace in such great and special measure, and to convey the nature and derivation of those feelings in a form recognisable to those who have known enthusiasm as I wished the word to be under-

* Cape, 1983.

stood, I found myself speculating more and more about the real meaning of the happiness that comes from friendship or Shakespeare, cats or books, cities or landscape, music or walking, paintings or stars, and from there I thought more and more of the greater brother of that happiness, the one that comes without any warning or even apparent cause, and can come as easily to the sick, the poor or the dying as to the successful, the healthy or the young, and perhaps more so.

Also to the middle-aged; which is where this excursion began. I wrote most of *Enthusiasms* in a room with a window above my desk, but set too high for me to see out of it without standing up. This was just as well; like all journalists, I find it unspeakably difficult to write without an imminent deadline, and – again like all my fellows – I will go to great lengths to seek distractions from the unwelcome task of actually putting words on paper, as opposed to thinking about doing so shortly. But the room was also small, bare and plain, and I conceived a fantasy in which I was a prisoner in an enlightened jail, allowed to work at my own trade and even to wander freely about the grounds in search of inspiration, returning thus refreshed to my labours, and soon began to imagine myself at work on such prison-written moral and didactic works as the *Consolations* of Boethius or *The Pilgrim's Progress*. From there, I fell to speculating about what it would be like to be a prisoner in reality instead of fantasy, and came to the astonishing and disturbing conclusion that provided I could read and write what I liked, and had a congenial cell-mate (or, better still, a sentence of solitary confinement), I would not find it nearly so terrible as I surely ought to.

This absurd belief was no doubt partly based on the fact that it *was* a fantasy and that I knew perfectly well it was; if the gates were really yawning open to admit me, let alone slamming shut behind me, I would no doubt sing a different tune. But I could not help feeling that that was a less than complete explanation, and sought long and carefully for the rest of it.

I was, after all, engaged in writing a book in which I was recounting the pleasures I derived from a wide variety of external sources; even the last chapter, which comes closest to describing the catch in the breath that comes from no discernible stimulus, takes as its starting-point a massively tangible work of art. Was I moving, even as I wrote, towards a different kind of pleasure altogether, the kind that is to be found only inside the human heart (however it got there) and that cannot be described, as a symphony or a wine can, a sunset or a mountain-top, architecture or literature? The Kingdom of Heaven, we are told, is within: suppose that were true, even if there is no such thing as the Kingdom of Heaven?

I was by then nearing the end of the book, and finished it with the satisfaction of knowing that there was indeed a book to be written which would start from where that one left off, though I might never write it. By now, however, eighteen months had passed, and I realised, without being able to say exactly why, that my long leave from regular journalism was coming to an end; I had embarked on it in April 1981, and returned to newspaper work in October 1982. But the refreshment and reinvigoration that I felt derived, I at once realised, from something far more significant than my long rest from tomorrow's deadline, or even from the fact that I had strictly kept my vow to cut the volume of work I was willing to undertake by fully two-thirds.

The title of this book is the phrase printed as a permanent heading on the column I now write for *The Times*; each article is followed by an ordinary headline which indicates the particular subject-matter dealt with. I cannot remember whether it was I or the Editor of *The Times* who suggested that such a 'strapline', as newspaper jargon calls it, might be employed, but the wording was my own suggestion; only after I had proposed it and it had been agreed did I realise that it meant, for me if not for the readers, more than it said.

It is highly undesirable, and anyway impossible, for any non-specialist journalist of comment to decide in advance on the kind of subject-matter he will write about (I am convinced that the reason *Punch* has always been dreadful and always will be is that its writers have to be funny every week, whereas nobody can be *anything* every week). If he is to interest his readers he must start by interesting himself, and unless he is impelled by that interest to put forward some thought or point of view, analysis or description, reaction or recommendation, praise or blame, he will always fail; for my own part, not only have I never, as a columnist, written anything for any reason other than that I had something that I wanted to say on the subject, but I do not know how I would go about writing anything if I did *not* want to say something on the subject.* My sabbatical, as I have said, began with the discovery that I did not feel impelled to say anything at all; plainly, I had embarked on it in the nick of time.

All the same, the very fact that I would be writing my *Times* column less than once a week, rather than the invariable thrice of my previous Ixion's wheel, meant that the nature of it would inevitably change. When producing three (and, incidentally, on the same three days of the week) I knew that I could, and indeed should, mix among the comments on the world's lunacies and brutalities, heroisms and nobilities, many comments on less weighty matters, from an account of a performance of an opera I had just seen or a meal I had just eaten, to a reminiscence of some bygone experience

* It should be obvious that in excluding specialist commentators from this rule I also exclude leader-writers; but theirs is an ability that I regard with a mixture of awe and terror.

or tale that had no purpose other than to amuse. *Dulce est desipere in loco*, and anyway I could return next day to British party politics or the sufferings of those who live under tyranny. (A fellow-columnist, who writes on a Sunday newspaper with a brief theoretically as wide as mine, once told me he envied my three shies at the coconut, because as he put it, 'I've got this black thing on my shoulder whispering in my ear, "This is your only contribution to Western civilisation for the next seven days – make it significant."')

I did not, knowing how dangerous it would be, *set out* to change my subject-matter; but I am sure it has in fact changed, and something in my subconscious must have signalled the change by hitting upon the title 'The Way We Live Now'. I feel far less often impelled to deal in the small change of party fortunes, to take sides in the quarrels of the eternally quarrelsome, even to labour in the vineyard of rebuking those who insist that twice two make five. But that is not the end of the matter, and is hardly even the beginning. That tired old cynic's jibe 'Five hundred years from now who'll know the difference?' has always struck me as the motto of the moribund; I have never met anyone I respect who used it. The most extraordinary fact about the physical universe is that it is indestructible; a speck of dust, a drop of water, a single breath – though they may change their form, rearrange the atoms of which they are made, become invisible even to the microscope's eye, they can never disappear. I am certain that even the trivia of our daily lives, the modish chatter of the empty-headed, the least thought of the thoughtless, the lightest word of the lightest mind, are similarly preserved, to be used (as anything at all can be used) on the universe's business if not on ours. That being so, I can and do take the stuff of my writing from wherever it may be found, and it should be obvious from what I have said about my methods that I do not, and cannot, seek it: it thrusts

itself on my attention, and I at once realise that there is
something I want to say about it.

Yet I have no doubt that I want to say less and less
about many of the subjects that once formed a substantial part of my stock-in-trade, and more and more about
themes that strike me as being relevant in a much wider
context. Any journalist who selects some of his newspaper work for book publication will find himself
discarding most of it; my own two earlier volumes were
selected, as I have said, from a decade's work, and
represented about a tenth of that decade's total (and
about 2 per cent of my entire output). The reason most
of it must be left to grow yellow and crumble is that it
deals with events and people long since forgotten, so
that comment on them would seem pointless even if it
were not incomprehensible. This book, however, is
drawn from a much smaller catchment area, and therefore represents a much higher proportion of it; the only
possible explanation is that the subjects to which I have
instinctively been drawn are of rather less ephemeral a
nature.

If that is so, I have no doubt it will continue to be so,
and that the tendency will increase. Whether this pleases
all or most of my readers I do not know; some of them
kindly write to tell me that it does, but I have no basis
on which to estimate how representative they are. But
even if I were convinced that most of my readers
deplore this development, there would be nothing I
could do about it, for the reasons I have given. (This
may be a good point at which to beg their pardon, and
also to make my regular declaration that although in
compiling this volume I have made a few excisions – of
now forgotten matter – and a few corrections of lapses
in style, punctuation, grammar or fact, I have changed
nothing at all in the views expressed.)

It must be obvious that 'the way we live now' means,
and is intended to mean, the way *it seems to me* we live

now. God forbid that I, or any other journalist, should set out consciously to paint a portrait of the times in ink that fades as fast as daily journalism. And yet if a journalist is consistent even as his outlook changes, he will find himself producing a recognisable portrait of the way he looks at the world. I could not for the life of me define, or even coherently describe, what *my* portrait of the world consists of, but I have no doubt that I am constantly drawing it, and that it will be found in this book. I hope there will be a successor volume in due course; there may be several. If so, I am sure that the portrait will be different even if the world remains the same, and that is unlikely enough; I am not the man I was, or the man I will be. No reader of this book will look at the way we live now with eyes that see exactly as mine do, for no reader of this book is me. Still, anyone who, having started the book, has got this far, must have found *something* recognisable in my exposition of what follows, and that shall be my excuse for concluding my Introduction with the traditional words: now read on.

April 1984   B.L.

The valley of dry bones

THERE WAS A strange and little-remarked story the other day which has been echoing in my head; not surprisingly, as it was composed almost entirely of echoes. It concerned bones, human bones, and a vast quantity of them – 50,000 was the figure mentioned. They came from a medieval burial ground at York; the area was being cleared for building, and the local archaeological trust was excavating the site before the owners – Sainsbury's, just to make the meeting of worlds more piquant – buried the whole thing, presumably under a supermarket. End of first echo.

The bones came from graves which were believed to be, though the documents were not ample enough for anyone to be quite sure, those of Jews; the area in which the cemetery lay, near York, was called Jewbury. Second echo; our century has seen Jewish bones produced in quantities never attained in all previous history, though (third, ironical, echo) the massacre of Jews at York in the twelfth century had more than a touch of the murderous frenzy that raged in civilised Europe less than fifty years ago.

The archaeologists, who wished to study and measure the bones to see what could be discovered about the people to whom they belonged, consulted the Chief Rabbi, Sir Immanuel Jakobovits. After considering such

1

evidence as the diggers had found, he asked them – and his wishes were at once met – to cease work on the examination of the bones and rebury them where they had been found. His reason was 'the reverence due to mortal remains which once bore the incomparable hallmark of the divine image, and which, we believe, have an inalienable right to stay undisturbed'. He added that 'dignity shown to human remains, even centuries after death, could contribute more than any scientific enquiry to human civilisation.'

Fourth echo: I have quoted the story from the pages of the *Guardian*, than which no newspaper today has a higher proportion of writers who would regard the Chief Rabbi's attitude as bizarre or perverse; I am sure, for instance, that Miss Polly Toynbee, who was recently waxing quite hysterical with relief at having found a nun who had not only left the convent but lost her faith on the way out, would not have the faintest idea of what the old boy was going on about, and for that matter precious little of what inspired the archaeologists' curiosity, her interest being limited to ensuring, when the Sainsbury's supermarket was erected on the site, that it would be amply stocked with muesli and un-sweetened yoghurt, and that *foie gras* and South African orange juice would be rigorously excluded from its shelves.

And yet it seems to me that something of great and enduring value in human civilisation is contained in the archaeologists' initial desire to examine the bones, in the Chief Rabbi's gently phrased appeal to them to desist, and in their ready willingness to relinquish their quest in what they recognised as a higher interest.

The archaeologists were driven by one of the noblest urges that civilised men and women can feel: the desire to join hands with the past and thus come closer to understanding both the past itself and what it can teach us about the present. When Schliemann sent his famous telegram, 'I have looked on the face of Agamemnon,' he was, as it transpired, mistaken; but the treasure he found at Mycenae was none the less far more valuable than the gold it was made of or the beauty of its workmanship, for it was a link with a story that has so far held captive the imagination of the world for twenty-eight centuries, and shows no sign at all of letting go.

So it was with Knossos, with Tutankhamun, with that amazing mosaic floor hard by Chichester, with the Ming Tombs of China, with every spadeful of earth carefully dug out of any archaeological site and examined carefully for evidence of the people who had preceded the diggers there, with Professor Glob and the bodies he kept finding, in a perfect state of preservation, beneath Denmark's watery soil, even with those splendid lunatics who burrowed their way into a hill beneath which they were convinced King Arthur was buried, and who emerged from the tunnel without Excalibur but with undiminished conviction.

I doubt if there is any such thing as a legend without some foundation in truth and history – no, not so much as Adam and Eve or Cinderella – and the desire to dig up even a single strand of evidence and patiently unravel it is one that should be, and is, admired by anybody with any imagination at all.

It is surely a measure of the York archaeologists' seriousness about their work that they so clearly understood and complied with the Chief Rabbi's wishes. All real archaeologists approach the past with the same attitude: reverence. The reverence is due to the past itself; if the diggers at York had found medieval kitchen utensils instead of bones they would have carried them no less carefully to their laboratory. But the reverence due to death, which was the Chief Rabbi's concern, intensifies the feeling of a meeting with the past, for it provides a link with a past that antedates the past itself, and must raise, in any mind not inextricably entangled in the belief that *nothing* 'could contribute more than any scientific enquiry to human civilisation', the question of why the dry bones once lived, and what breathed the life into them.

The reverence accorded to death is one of the oldest and most powerful ideas in human beings – so old, indeed, and so deeply embedded in so many societies, that it is hard to resist the conclusion that it must be biological; it would be as surprising to find an era or a culture that did not surround death with elaborate and profound beliefs and rituals as it would be to find a race of men with three legs. Some societies bury their dead, some burn them, some mummify and preserve them, some even eat them; all, however, start and finish with the same attitude, which is that in the presence of death we are as close as may be to solving the riddle of life, and it is therefore fitting that we should approach it in a spirit of awe. Why, of all the miracles, is it the raising of Lazarus that is the most powerful in its effect on our imagination and feelings? Because it cancelled the most uncancellable of debts, reversed the most irreversible of movements, denied the most palpable of proofs; if this man can annul death, then surely he is no man at all, and will one day annul his own.

So it is with the bones at York, and the truth that the Chief Rabbi seized upon. There is an instinct in us all that he encapsulated when he spoke of 'the reverence due to mortal remains which once bore the incomparable hallmark of the divine image', and added that 'the dignity shown to human remains' was a mark of true civilisation. One of the greatest terrors that haunts any deathbed is that of the casual or contemptuous disposal of the dying one's body. Our modern 'rationalists' would smile at something so primitive and superstitious as the belief that a dead body could matter to its previously living owner, and would never seek to enquire, however rationally, where the belief comes from, and why it is so strong. But that, after all, is why I have put 'rationalists' in quotation marks.

No one can now match a name or a face to a single bone of the great ossuary found at York. But it is not necessary to do so; it is necessary only to remember that those dead bones were once clad in flesh, and at once the mystery of life itself springs from the ground to confront us.

I saw a man die: he was a London bricklayer's labourer with seven children. He left seventeen pounds club money; and his wife spent it all on his funeral and went into the workhouse with the children next day. She would not have spent sevenpence on her children's schooling: the law had to force her to let them be taught gratuitously; but on death she spent all she had.

That passage is from *Man and Superman,* and it puts the opposite case very well. Those who know the play, however, will recall that the speaker is the Devil. The Chief Rabbi, and the York Archaeological Trust, know better, and those bones may now sleep soundly, undisturbed by the trolleys of Sainsbury's customers, until they wake never to sleep again.

The Times January 11th, 1984

General principles, private lives

She was poor but she was honest,
Victim of the squire's game,
First 'e loved 'er, then 'e left 'er,
And she lost 'er 'onest name.

THE ONE FIGURE in l'affaire Parkinson for whom I have no sympathy at all is Mr William Deedes, Editor of the *Daily Telegraph*. I could have told him (but he didn't ask me) that the gentle irony of his paper's leading article ('. . . the moral logic . . . that a quiet abortion is greatly to be preferred to a scandal . . . hardly seems a moral advance') was, like all irony, a weapon more dangerous to the hand wielding it than to anyone against whom it might be directed. It took Miss Keays a mere three days to work out a method of misunderstanding it (the technique included excising the last sentence altogether), and there she was, as white as Mother Teresa of Calcutta. How much better to be the Editor of the *Daily Mirror*, who claims that when two of his reporters confronted Miss Keays last August she refused to comment but told them 'your manner has been most polite'. (The *Mirror*'s Editor is far too modest; what she actually said to the men she found on her doorstep, not to say colliding with her car, was: 'Please allow me to commend the tact and discretion with which you have conducted yourselves, for you both stand four-square in the finest traditions of the British popular press; not for nothing, evidently, is the motto of your great newspaper *Honor est praemium virtutis*. I thank you from the bottom of my heart, in which there will always be a warm corner for two such *preux chevaliers*, surely the Roland and Oliver of Fleet Street.')

> See 'er riding in 'er kerridge,
> In the Park, all brave and gay:
> All the nibs and nobby persons
> Come to pass the time of day.

Then – while we are still clearing the undergrowth in preparation for the autumn sowing – there was Miss Keays's friend and confidante, Mrs Colvin, who assured the *Daily Mail*, in discussing the statement which, published in the middle of the Conservative Party Conference, brought Mr Parkinson down, that 'The timing was not significant and I'm certain she had no intention of causing Cecil and the Government the maximum of embarrassment.' The cynical may jeer, but my own researches have revealed that Miss Keays was not even aware that the Conference was going on, indeed she did not know that Mr Parkinson was a leading government minister, having been under the impression that he was either Professor Parkinson of Parkinson's Law, or Michael Parkinson of television fame, and was astonished to discover in what circles she had been moving, though not so astonished as she was when she learned too late that babies – contrary to the belief she had held all her life – are not found under gooseberry bushes.

> In the rich man's arms she flutters,
> Like a bird with broken wing;

7

First 'e loved 'er, then 'e left 'er,
And she 'asn't got no ring.

As for Mr Parkinson, he seems to have established a novel principle for the ordering of his domestic arrangements, viz., that he decides to share his life with whichever lady has spoken sharply to him most recently; I suppose it's a mercy that after the dramatic 2 am meeting in the Thatchers' Blackpool suite he didn't announce that he was going to elope with the Prime Minister.

Finally, there is the Bishop of Bath and Wells. I must say firmly that I am sick and tired of clergymen meddling in matters which are none of their concern; an English Bishop's duties, in the field of public comment, are to denounce NATO, complain that the levels of Supplementary Benefit are too low and demand that there should be no cuts in NHS funding, not to go about pronouncing on questions of morality, which are entirely outwith a clergyman's competence and should be left to newspaper columnists.*

As far as this newspaper columnist is concerned, no moral view of the rights and wrongs of the private relationship between Mr Parkinson and Miss Keays will be expressed. She has taken her revenge, and although it is my belief that vengeance is at once the most sterile and most corrosive of all human pursuits, not even excluding war itself, she is not obliged to share my view, and in any case neither I nor anyone else other than the two people concerned can know enough of what happened between them to be able to pronounce with episcopal confidence where justice lies, or indeed what, in this context, it consists of.

But because Mr Parkinson is a politician and was a Cabinet minister, the affair inevitably takes on a diffe-

---

* Hoist with my own petard. This irony was taken as seriously by many of my readers as was Mr Deedes's by his.

rent aspect, and a different kind of question can be asked: what is, and what should be, the relationship between a public man's public life and his private life? That question, by one of those immutable laws of history that Sir Karl Popper so unwisely scorns, is asked every ten years in this country. It was asked in 1963, the *annus horribilis* that began at Cliveden and ended with a new Prime Minister; in 1973, when the focus of attention was not a stately home but a house of ill-fame in the Maida Vale; and now once more; I wonder whose turn it will be in 1993? (It won't be Gummer, anyway, thank God.)

There is an unspoken premise (it is unspoken because if it were to be spoken it would at once collapse under the weight of its own absurdity) that politicians must be subject to more stringent rules of personal conduct than the rest of us because they are 'looked up to' and must therefore 'set an example'. Countless millions of would-be sinners, it seems, are held in check by the thought that if the Minister of State at the Department of the Environment and Local Government would never make a pass at the *au pair* it would ill become lesser mortals to do so, and that if, on the other hand, the Parliamentary Under-Secretary to the Ministry of Agriculture and Fisheries should in the absence of his wife be found in the attic, trouserless and not alone, it will signal to the nation that all standards have been abolished and the very beasts of the field are no longer safe from the effects of human depravity.

I am, as is well known, much given to hyperbole in the course of making a point with emphasis. I must therefore make clear that I am not employing this useful device when I say that in all my life I have never met any persons, in any trade or profession, whether educated or uneducated, sophisticated or naive, rich or poor, old, young or middle-aged, who would seek objective standards of moral behaviour, against which to measure

9

their own, from our political leaders, or who would find otherwise than ridiculous or unintelligible the thought that they should.

> See 'im in the 'ouse of Commons,
> Passin' laws to put down crime,
> While the girl that 'e 'as ruined
> Picks 'er way through mud and slime.

Note that the public-morality nonsense applies only to politicians; captains of industry may swap wives without being obliged to leave office, and of actors it seems positively expected that they should. Of course, those who are *ex officio* charged with the care of souls, like bishops, or with literally laying down the law, like judges, must observe certain rules that do not apply to the rest of us, because something real and important would be damaged if too many of them fell too conspicuously from grace. But that is the price a man pays for wearing a full-bottomed wig or lawn sleeves; who started the rumour that politicians are in a similar position, and whoever he was, why didn't he notice that it isn't true?

The politicians are themselves very substantially to blame. The way so many of them – most, I think – behave in the scramble to put those two magic letters after their name has had the effect of elevating their trade so far above the generality of mankind that it has taken on a spurious but superficially plausible appearance of purity and nobility. This is dangerously enhanced by the way MPs tend to talk about the House of Commons; anyone who has ever heard them, towards the end of a debate on some matter of national importance, congratulating themselves on the high seriousness with which they have approached the matter in their speeches, will know exactly what the word *hubris* means. Indeed, I believe that the prurient public interest in political scandals (demanded of, and supplied by, the press) is largely based on a healthy understanding of the mythical quality of the politicians' collective view of themselves and their function, and the relish with which a politician's fall is received is attributable to the doubt-less deplorable, but surely understandable, feeling that the pride that goeth before a fall makes the fall not only inevitable but deserved.

> When they dragged 'er from the river,
> Water from 'er clothes they wrung,
> For they thought that she was drownded,
> But the corpse sat up and sung –

It is surely ironic beyond the dreams of the *Daily Telegraph* leader-writers that Britain, the originator of representative parliamentary government, should be afflicted more than any other nation with the claim that public men are different from private ones. Democracy wouldn't even work if that were true, if we selected our political representatives from some pool of special beings resembling Miss Beale and Miss Buss (' . . . how different from us'), for we must be able to see ourselves mirrored in our politicians; as I have said more than once, in a democracy we are all politicians, and the day we forget it will be a black day for us all. We do not have to hold in view the hideous fate of the MP who in savagely moral terms denounced the central figure of the 1963 events, only to be revealed years later as a paid parliamentary hireling of Mr Poulson; it is not always true, after all, that those who are most zealous in the reproof of vice are whited sepulchres themselves. But we do have to remember that it is inevitable for our politicians to suffer from the same frailties as the rest of us, because they are the same people as the rest of us; the truth about public men is that they are only private men whose lives are lived in public.

11

Mr Parkinson had to resign when he did, for two reasons. First, he had become an embarrassment and a liability to the Government; however he got into that position, it was thus, and the consequences inevitably followed. But the second reason was firmly rooted in the ancient hypocrisy: in the false and tainted assumption that a politician's loves or lusts are more culpable than those of a butcher, a baker or a candlestick-maker. They are not, but too many politicians have wanted the public to think too well of them, and too many newspapers have cashed in on the proposition's fallacy; the result can be seen in the outer darkness into which Mr Parkinson has now been cast. One day we shall all grow out of it; we shall be able to see a domestic tragedy for no more and no less than what it is, and to evince no pretended surprise that it should have taken place around a politician. I don't know what the mass-circulation papers will do for a living then, but that is not my problem. Let us resolve to remember that the world and its inhabitants are not perfect, and are most unlikely to become perfect by next Friday. Meanwhile, it must remain true, alas, that people who live in glass houses should undress in the dark.

– It's the rich what 'as the pleasure,
It's the poor what gets the blame,
It's the same the 'ole world over
Ain't it all a bleedin' shame?

The Times   October 17th, 1983

Fight the good fight

THERE IS A Church of England parish – let us call it, lest I should unwittingly add fuel to flames already liberally supplied therewith, by the name of the Reverend Alan Bennett's celebrated incumbency, St Jack-in-the-Lifeboat – in which all is not well between the shepherd and his flock.

The trouble began when the vicar proposed that the collection should be taken during the last hymn of the service, when, as he put it, 'the coin rattling and foot shuffling would be drowned'.

This, you may think, would be a logical step. The organist, however, saw it far otherwise; until now, the collection had always been taken during the sermon, and as far as he was concerned, it should continue to be. In the report of this unhappy business that I have seen, the organist is not quoted as drawing the appallingly obvious inference – that the drowning of the sermon in a sea of coin rattling and foot shuffling would be a less serious matter than the drowning of the accompaniment to a hymn – but none could deny that such an inference is hovering over the pulpit.

The vicar maintained his position, the organist his. Deadlock ensued, broken by the dismissal of the latter, presumably by the former. The vicar, it seemed, was at last in a position to deliver his sermons untroubled by the rattle of a single widow's mite or the shuffling of the smallest infant toe. The Hosts of Midian (or, depending which view of the matter you take, the Defenders of the Faith) were not, however, to be denied; the choir, all twenty of them, promptly downed psalters and came out on strike. This left the vicar uninterrupted, but the interruptions unhymned; a new deadlock ensued, and the Bishop was called in. What His Lordship said to the warring parties history does not record, but shortly afterwards the vicar went on holiday, the organist was deemed 'suspended', and all the Bishop would say for public consumption was: 'The situation is a very delicate one.'

I dare say, and made more so by a disquieting new note struck by a spokesman for the disaffected choir. 'The vicar', he declared, 'is trying to introduce high church practices here which we dislike.'

Here I must make a personal disclaimer. I would rather put my head into the mouth of a lion in the Roman arena than get mixed up in a dispute over the height of Christian church doctrine or ritual; in these matters I am a paid-up, card-carrying, lifelong Latitudinarian, and a Jewish one to boot. I took no part in the Reformation or Counter-Reformation, I have never been heard to express a preference for *homoiousian* over *homoousian*, or vice versa, and anyone claiming to know my views on the place in Christian belief of confession, purgatory or candlesticks should be treated as an impostor. What is more, I am quite unable to see how the timing of the collection in a church could give rise to any question of orthodoxy or heterodoxy anyway, irrespective of the merits of the rival factions' claims to be the only guardians of the true faith.

But this makes me more, not less, confident of being able to pronounce upon the troubles at St Jack's. For whether the trouble there is concerned with the introduction of high church practices, or whether it is more

14

in the nature of an industrial dispute, I have to tell the
faithful to be not dismayed; it is quarrels of this kind, in
parishes of this kind, which prove not only that the
heart of the Anglican Church is still beating soundly in
the body of the country it was born in, but that that
country is itself still undamaged, unchanged and un-
sinkable. 'Rightly to be great', said Hamlet,

> Is not to stir without great argument,
> But greatly to find quarrel in a straw,
> When honour's at the stake.

But the parishioners and clergy of that amazing
institution, the Church of England, can and do find
quarrel in a straw when *nothing's* at the stake, and those
who believe that such an attitude shows that their
church means nothing to them have got the matter
upside down, inside out and back to front: it is precisely
because they care so passionately for every blade of
grass in the churchyard and every fold in the vicar's
surplice that these weird and inexplicable dissensions
arise among them, and it is because their faith is so deep
and to them so clear, and therefore so rarely troubled by
doctrinal dissension, that a disagreement over the best
moment for the collection can turn into a battle of wills
that splits the parish and leads to charges of high-
handedness mingled with romanism and heresy. Come:
is it not better for the choir to go on strike and the vicar
to go on holiday than for both of them to go on an
expedition in search of Albigensians to exterminate? Is it
not better for the organist to cut the vicar dead than for
him to pray to God to strike him dead? Is it not better
for the Mothers' Union to bake loaves for the Harvest
Festival than (as will soon be happening if some of our
more *engagé* clergy have their way) to knit woollen
hand-grenade covers for the Khmer Rouge?

We are, on the whole, an extraordinarily unwarlike

and unexcitable nation. I believe that the failure of totalitarian political groups of both right and left to make headway with any substantial number of voters is only partly due to the voters' distaste for dictatorship and tyranny; it is also based on a profound and healthy abhorrence of systems which would inevitably entail Englishmen hitting other Englishmen over the head. Englishmen do, of course, hit other Englishmen over the head; but look why they do it. They do it in the course of quarrels about beer or football or one another's wives or, at the very worst, in the course of trying to steal one another's wallets. To suggest that they might take to doing it in the course of political disagreement would be regarded as a most outlandish idea, and the thought that they might do it in a religious cause would be incomprehensible to the point of embarrassment.

Long may it remain thus. The parishioners of St Jack-in-the-Lifeboat will be accused by the short-sighted of a failure in their sense of proportion. But surely they have displayed a sense of proportion of supreme delicacy and wisdom; they have quarrelled over things that do not matter, and have thus ensured that they will not be impelled to do each other harm, rather than – as with the Irish, to go no further for examples – over things that do matter, thus allowing themselves to be led into cursing one another's souls or murdering one another's bodies.

'If anyone speaks of religion in England,' said Montesquieu, 'everyone laughs.' That is perfectly true, but the Frenchman had missed the point. The laughter is directed at those who think it necessary to *speak* of religion, a practice to which foreigners are much given but which the English rightly think unnecessary. I will wager that even now they are not talking of religion in the streets of St Jack-in-the-Lifeboat. For what has happened there is that something disagreeable has been *injected into* the practice of their religion; the talk will be of organists and clergymen, choirs and collections, while beneath the talk their religion will continue to flow untroubled and unremarked. How the quarrel between the vicar and the choir is to be resolved I do not know; nor, apparently, does the Bishop. But we may be sure that the solution will be as English as the problem, and that not a drop of blood will be spilt in the course of it.

The Times   June 20th, 1983

Ambassador Extraordinary

I HAVE BEEN to see *From Mozart to Mao*, the film about Isaac Stern's visit to China. As it chances, by the time you read these words I shall be on my way to New York to see Isaac himself, and the first thing I shall do when we meet is to throw my arms round him (or as far round him as they will go) and tell him that the film is not only a memorable account of a musical triumph combined with a penetrating and absorbing view of Chinese society, but a joyful and poetic experience which, in the lifting of the spirits that it gives, resembles the effect of music itself.

The Chinese authorities invited the violinist to make a concert tour of their country, but they got a very great deal more than they bargained for, not only in the shape of the film (I gather that something like a hundred hours of material was shot, from which the hour and a half that it lasts was edited), but in the way the tour became an astonishing meeting of musical minds. Stern played, taught, talked, asked, demonstrated, joked, criticised, praised and above all threw himself with all his considerable vigour into the life of China; the Chinese responded at every level, and threw themselves no less vigorously into experiencing the life of this outstanding player, a man, as well as a musician, in a million.

The chief visible quality of Isaac Stern is his benignity. This is not the gentle benignity of our dear Yehudi, who really wants nothing at all except to communicate his devotion to music and make everybody in the world love one another (he has so far succeeded only in the first of these two laudable ambitions),* it is a demanding, provoking, zestful outpouring of a Greatheart's vitality, for if Isaac Stern has a motto it is surely taken from the *andante maestoso* of Beethoven's Ninth Symphony:

> *Seid umschlungen, Millionen:*
> *Diesen Kuss der ganzen Welt!*

It is this quality that gives the film its characteristic tone, and that must have made the Chinese authorities occasionally feel like the hunter who cried: 'I have caught a bear, but he won't let me go.' There is, for instance, an instructive and fascinating moment early in the film when Stern makes clear that there are bones beneath the *embonpoint*; he is talking to a group of musicians about Mozart, and the *apparatchik* assigned to the meeting says that the explanation of Mozart is that he was a product of the emerging capitalist society. Menuhin would have had a massive internal haemorrhage but kept smiling; Stern, with infinite gentleness and courtesy, made clear that he had never heard such disgusting rubbish in the whole of his life.

Isaac Stern's passion for communication through music was seen at its best in the work he did with the Chinese children who crowd the film from beginning to end. He teased them, showed them, encouraged them, hugged them, praised them – in a word, inspired them; I will wager a very large sum that the little pig-tailed

---

*This passage is open to misunderstanding; I was not suggesting that Mr Menuhin was some kind of musical dreamer. The school he founded is only one example of his notable work off the concert platform.

nine-year-old to whom he gave an impromptu lesson has slept ever since with a photograph of him under her pillow. And the audiences, whether of children and students in the musical academies he visited, or in the packed concert halls in which he played, were visibly rapt throughout – when, that is, they were not convulsed with laughter as he pantomimed a joke with his exceptionally voluble hands.

So this beautiful and moving travelogue continues, with Stern infecting all those he meets with his happy devotion to music and his happy curiosity about everyone and everything he comes upon. (He visits the training school for those astounding acrobats we have seen in the West, and watches, turned to stone with amazement, as a girl fends off with her feet a series of wooden staves thrown at her, with increasing rapidity, by four colleagues simultaneously; her agility and grace, and the sheer impossibility of what she was doing, made me, only a few minutes after the scene had ended, wonder whether I had not imagined it. Stern, when it was over, found the perfect line with which to celebrate the return of his ability to speak: 'On the other hand,' he said, '*they* can't play Mozart.')

And then, without warning, the darkness descends; the abruptness of the change is almost as shocking as the change itself. Towards the end of the tour, in Shanghai, Stern is summing up his impressions. He expresses surprise at one aspect of Chinese music-making that he has found everywhere; the younger children, from eight to eleven or thereabouts, are plainly very talented, giving great promise for the future, but the older ones – from fifteen to nineteen, say – have lost the fine edge of quality. What has happened in between?

I don't know whether Stern knew the answer before he asked the question; if he did not, it must have struck him an almost mortal blow. The *apparatchik*, human for once, gave the official explanation first: the stamping-out of all Western influence during the Cultural Revolution meant that an entire generation of young Chinese musicians, forbidden to continue with their studies, had had their formative years stolen from them; the older students Stern had heard were of this group, the younger ones, now that the prohibition on Western music had been lifted, would continue to advance.

But that was only the explanation, and it was given in terms much less stark than my paraphrase: what did the explanation really mean? Its full meaning was revealed by the Deputy Director of the Shanghai Conservatory, clearly a man of great sweetness and quality; slowly and quietly, in excellent English, he described the murderous lunacy of the Cultural Revolution, with the Red Guards acting as the storm-troopers of a movement that was, in its hatred of civilisation in every form, literally Nazi in character. Ten of the professors at the Conservatory had committed suicide; not, this gentle sage said, because of the incessant beatings and torture, which could be borne, but because of the degradation and humiliation that were visited upon them.

He described his own. For fourteen months he had been confined to a cupboard under the stairs, without light or ventilation, and with a septic tank beneath the floorboards; he was allowed out for only a few minutes a day. It was clear that, even by the insane proscriptions of the time, he had committed no crime except the ultimate crime of loving the art he taught; as an extra punishment for it, he was allowed, throughout the whole period of his torment, a single visit from his daughter and grandchild, *lasting five minutes*.

The Chinese rulers, though they have posthumously demoted Mao from his position of God-King, are not yet ready to criticise him seriously, let alone to admit that the Gang of Four was a Gang of Five, and that the terror was unleashed by him. Still, the elderly professor spoke with a very remarkable openness, not least in

21

making clear the reason for the brutalities at his Conservatory, plainly typical of what was happening throughout the country. (Anyone who sees this extraordinary film might do well, when this scene is reached, to remember – indeed, it would be hard not to – that while this dreadful mania was raging throughout China, there were plenty of voices raised in praise of it in Britain and elsewhere in the West).

A film filled with such heart and happiness cannot be allowed to end on such a note. Over a rapid montage of brief scenes we hear repeated the old professor's final words: 'I do not think such times will come again,' and then we are back finally in the concert hall, as Stern sweeps to the end of the Brahms Concerto, with the whole audience exploding in excitement and gratitude. This film won an Oscar in the documentary category; it deserves also a prize for its contribution to understanding, to art, to civilisation and to humanity itself.

The Times   April 4th, 1983

Abominable Snow man

Stranger and Brother: A Portrait of C.P. Snow by Philip Snow*

THIS IS A very odd book. The author is the younger of the two surviving brothers of the subject, and himself a writer in a small way (his *Cricket in the Fiji Islands* is doubtless an indispensable work for those interested in cricket in the Fiji Islands). Clearly, he loved and hero-worshipped his better-known sibling; the last words of the book are ' . . . it is nearly two years since Charles's death and I am bereft.'

Yet the portrait he has, all unconsciously, painted is of a monster: selfish, vain, grasping and foolish. Was Snow such a man? I cannot say; the only contact I ever had with him arose from an action for libel he brought against me for suggesting, more clumsily than is my wont, that he was a fellow-traveller, which is hardly the best vantage-point for forming an estimate of a man's character. On the other hand, who could be better equipped for the task than a brother? And if this is what a brother thinks he was like, what worse could a stranger say?

'His letters', says Snow minor at the beginning of a chapter that is almost entirely composed of them, 'tell

*Macmillan, 1982.

23

The Way We Live Now

us a lot about him.' He then kicks off with one which, if any brother of mine had written it to me on October 13th, 1938, I would have hastened to burn:

> I don't think there is now any chance of a major war in Europe for years . . . it is more likely that Fascism will spread, quickly and fairly quietly, over France and England, beginning with an increase of censorship and ending with anti-semitism . . . It will probably happen . . . inside the next three years. Fascism has won . . . it will last our lifetimes. There is no one to fight against it . . . My own course is entirely a matter of timing. I must get the first book . . . out early next year in the US . . . after that I retire to California . . . I shall go across . . . next summer and stay more or less by accident.

This combination of political nonsense and an eye to the main chance sets the tone for much of the book, but even more repellent are Snow's accounts of his relations with women:

> I deliberately didn't see Rachel again: I daren't get entangled with a woman just now: it's better to travel light. If I make any money in America, and there seems no immediate chance of the US going the same way as England, then I may look round for a wife. One Saturday night . . . I sent for Rosie from Nottingham and had a distinctly satisfactory champagnerous Edwardian sort of night. Jack [Plumb] can't understand this . . .

Nor, I dare say, could Rosie, nor Rachel, nor S, nor J – nor A:

> His will included a provision for his post-war secretary, Anne Seagrim. Charles had resumed in 1957 his

24

close relationship with Anne Seagrim, broken off in 1950 before his marriage to Pam. The existence of this relationship did not bring about any estrangement between Charles and Pam, and indeed Pam was unaware of it.

Surely 'and indeed' should read 'because'? The attitude appears to be catching, yet the author remains apparently ignorant of the effect he is having on the reader, as he shows his brother as a man for whom other human beings were no more than extensions of his own ego.

Enough of Snow in bed; what of Snow at his desk? His novelist's desk, that is: his brief and ridiculous career as the back legs of a pantomime horse at the Ministry of Technology (the front legs were played by Frank Cousins, and two more weirdly over-parted Ministers can never have held office) is mentioned, but not described, though the imp at the author's elbow persuades him to repeat Snow's estimate of Harold Wilson: 'quite abnormally impressive – more so than any Western politician I have met'.

Possibly Snow as a writer will be best remembered as the subject of a still-echoing attack by Leavis; certainly, his plodding novels (the author reveals that hardly any principal character in any of them was created, Snow having simply taken colleagues, friends, relatives and acquaintances and made his books out of them) are without any serious or lasting quality. His own view of his literary talent was that it deserved both the OM and Nobel Prize; he compared himself to Stendhal, and several times seemed on the brink of comparing himself to Tolstoy as well, though since Richard Church compared him to Dostoevsky and Richard Aldington to Proust, I suppose he can hardly be blamed for his good conceit of himself. (He collected honorary degrees the way even sillier men collect stamps.)

Snow's intimate and mutually admiring friendship

The Way We Live Now

with Mikhail Sholokhov, a Stalinist (and Khrushchevist, and Brezhnevist) toady who publicly called for the dissident writers Sinyavsky and Daniel to be shot, was perhaps the most staining episode in his life, another fact of which his artless brother seems to be quite unaware, as indeed he seems to be of what this vignette reveals:

> Pam's arthritic mother, carrying coal from the cellar . . . to the drawing room, would often find the door punctiliously held open for her by Charles, but it would never have occurred to him to relieve her of the coal bucket itself . . .

At one moment, we see Snow trying to dissuade his brother from seeking a career in cricket administration; next moment, we discover that this is because he is thinking of buying a tax-loss farm, and wants Philip to manage it for him. Then he says he wants to make the author's leave (from the Colonial Service) more comfortable, 'so will you take a house at my expense and charge the upkeep to me?' In the next sentence we discover the reason for this generosity: 'It would be nice if you and Anne could do some entertaining for me.' A man who wants to use his brother as a bailiff in the country and a butler in town must figure high on anyone's list of people it is pleasant not to have known, but the author remains innocent from beginning to end.

Macmillan's should look to their editing; disinterested is not the same as uninterested, nor eupeptic as euphoric, and what is meant by 'Buddha's impermeability' I cannot imagine – I never heard anyone complain that Buddha let the rain in. Nor is the novel sequence of 'Strangers and Brothers' 'the longest in literary history', for there are also 11 of Upton Sinclair's Lanny Budd chronicles and 27 volumes in Jules Romains's *Les Hommes de bonne volonté*. And the index is useless.

Observer   October 24th, 1982

Consequences

MARX SURELY PROVIDES one of the greatest paradoxes of history. Nearly half the people in the world live under governments that call themselves Marxist, and although the ultimate goal of humanity, in Marx's philosophy, was the freeing of the individual from the bonds of class and exploitation which had held him since the rise of capitalism, a process of liberation which was to end with the withering away of the state, every one of the regimes which profess to live by his system is a brutal tyranny, in which the individual is less free than any capitalist wage-slave and in which the state, so far from withering away, is more obtrusive, more powerful and more ruthless than any government based on the class system.

How are we to explain this extraordinary looking-glass world? One way is to say – what is certainly true – that none of these 'Marxist' governments have anything Marxist about them, and that if Marx could return and examine them he would be quite unable to understand how and why his name had been dragged into the matter. But of course that explanation, so far from clearing up the mystery, makes it all the more obscure. For if the Marxists have lost their Marxism, wherewith shall they be Marxed? Why should a Russian government in 1983 feel obliged to pretend that it rules by the

27

principles laid down in (the phrase is from Ian Mackay)
a big, boring book on Victorian economics written by
an old man with a beard in Tufnell Park? None of the
rulers concerned has ever read the book; they couldn't
have done, for no one could possibly finish it, not even
Marx, who gave up, bored insensible by his own
rubbish, after the first volume, though he lived on for
more than a decade, sponging off Engels intellectually
as well as financially, and leaving him to make what he
could of the rest of the book.

This particular part of the Marxist legacy has many
sides. The very same fate, it can be seen, has overtaken
Trotsky, our own world being awash with idiots who
call themselves Trotskyites without having read, let
alone understood, a line of their hero *or* of Marx: for
that matter the murderous lunacy called Maoism gave
rise to a similar following elsewhere, calling themselves
Maoist to the genuine bewilderment of the Chinese
leadership, who could discern nothing of their ruler's
views in those held by many who styled themselves his
loyal subjects *in partibus infidelium.*

A theory which, whatever its deviser's intentions, has
given rise to *nothing* but a barbaric despotism must
surely have had something wrong with it in the first
place. What is the *causal* connexion between Marx's
Marxism and the pseudo-Marxism of the Soviet
empire, between a theory of liberation and an actuality
of slavery, between a Utopian idealist who wanted all
men to be brothers and a gallery of thugs who want
nothing but the perpetuation of their own power?

I put it like that because of all the excuses for
communist tyranny to be heard in the West one of the
most repulsive, as well as the feeblest, is the claim that it
cannot be laid to the door of Marx, or indeed of Lenin
(who, it should be remembered, set up the Gulag). But
in law, a man is held to be responsible for the likely
consequences of his actions, and certainly it is not

difficult to find in those of Marx and Marxism the seeds of the still proliferating evil practised in their name.

To start with, a man as personally intolerant as Marx, who was constantly denouncing and excommunicating all those in his own camp who ventured to question some detail of his argument, can hardly keep intolerance out of the bones of his philosophy. He did not have the power to send those he anathematised to their death, but he offered to those who came later a ready-made set of templates from which the justification of millions of deaths could be constructed, and it is no use saying he did not intend it; maybe not, but he *was* it.

He was also, in the same sense, the dictatorship of the proletariat, one of the greatest individual paradoxes within the main paradox itself: there is no system of government in the world, no, not the most corrupt personal fief of the worst of Black Africa's dictators, in which the proletariat have less say in their own destiny than in the lands of communism, *né* Marxism. But it is all too easy for those who dictate to the proletariat, by combining Rousseau (the father of modern totalitarianism) with Marx, to persuade themselves that all they are doing is to carry out the proletariat's dictatorship by a form of representative government; Rousseau allows such rulers to claim that the proletariat, if they knew their best interests, would approve, and Marx provides a set of principles for the dictatorships to rule by. And the gun and the barbed wire will take care of anyone who points out that on both counts the emperor has no clothes.

The next charge that can be laid to Marx's account is his historicism; again, the charge is not so much that he was guilty of it, though obviously he was, as that those who came after used it to justify their own crimes, so that Marx faces judgment as an accessory before the fact. If history is seen as a consistent progress through definable stages of development towards an ultimate apotheosis in which 'pre-history ends and history begins', then anyone who tries to push history out of its orbit must be an enemy of the people, for whom no fate can be too harsh; from this point it is no great step to arguing that anyone who denies that history is still in its original orbit is an enemy of the people too. Meanwhile the ultimate apotheosis is indefinitely postponed, no doubt through the machinations of more enemies of the people, who must be sought out all the more ruthlessly, and all the more ruthlessly punished, even if the effort required for such salutary action means that the apotheosis must wait even longer.

But finally, and most important, there is the principle most closely associated with Marx, though Engels, faced with the realisation that it was manifest nonsense, tried to weasel out of it after Marx's death: historical materialism. And it is that nonsense, which five minutes' conversation with a single real human being would push over, that constitutes the greatest crime committed by this harbinger of slavery and murder. Once the rulers are possessed of a theory which purports to explain *everything* in terms outside both the explainers and the explained-to, human beings become objects in a theory, and if there is one thing we know about objects in a theory, it is that they do not feel pain, not even from rubber truncheons or bullets. QED.

Lenin, Stalin, Brezhnev, Ulbricht, Jaruzelski, Rakosi, Mao, Castro – such men as these are not aberrations from Marxism, but its most perfect flowers, its juiciest fruits. Marxism gave them the weapons, and they finished the job; the fact that they finished Marxism at the same time is the last great irony of the story, but it is no consolation to those who died or to those who rot in jail, or for that matter to those who still live still free and wish to stay that way. The revolution envisaged in the *Communist Manifesto* is, in the communist lands, further off than ever. No doubt that distresses Marx as much as it surprises him. But he has no one to blame except himself.

The Times March 11th, 1983

A Europe of our dreams

M R HAROLD MACMILLAN, by all accounts, was in uncommonly good fettle at the Carlton Club on Tuesday night, giving, by popular demand, a performance of his justly celebrated Greeks-in-the-Roman-Empire (or possibly the Holborn Empire) number, and looking forward to the birth of a new Europe, not necessarily in wedlock.

I sometimes think that the minds of men are shaped more by the war they lived through than by any other influence. For me, and I suspect for very many of my generation, the Second World War became so crucial and formative an experience (I was eleven when it started) that all the succeeding years have telescoped, and continue to do so, into a single dawn; I cannot rid myself of the habit of saying 'before the war', and only when I say it to one of my grown-up godchildren and see the wondering look that it provokes do I realise that 'before the war' means no more to their feelings than 'Henry the Eighth had six wives'. I am sure that for millions of Americans the Vietnam war will have the same effect, and they in their turn will meet a generation for whom Hue will be one with San Juan Hill, and will find themselves obliged to come to terms with their instinctive indignation at such misprision of 'their' war. (I fear, however, that it is too much to hope that Mr

Michael Foot will ever give up trying to stop the Labour Party conference going out to lunch by announcing that the Spanish Civil War is still raging and Franco is at the gates of Madrid, though for anyone younger than Manny Shinwell the Crossing of the Ebro is likely to be thought a reference to Moses leading the Jews through the Red Sea.)

And so it is, and even more so, with Mr Macmillan. More so because he fought in the First World War, and saw his generation cut down around him. For him 'before the war' is even more poignant than for me, since he really can remember a Europe without passports, indeed almost without frontiers, when it was possible to think of western Europe as one civilisation:

The western world has not made the progress that when I was young we dreamed of: indeed Europe has not been what we meant it to be. It has not become a confederation of all the civilized powers that remain, with a single military policy, a single economic policy, a single monetary policy. It would have been a counterbalance to the powers we face, and it hasn't happened.

That passage alone dates Mr Macmillan to within a decade. Europe a nation! I know of no nobler dream, nor one less likely to be experienced waking. All sorts and conditions of men have been attracted to it, from Charlemagne to Jean Monnet; de Gaulle talked of 'l'Europe des patries', and Desmond Donnelly spoke of 1914–18 and 1939–45 as 'the two European Civil Wars'. What else is the EEC but the same dream? What was the idea, scuppered by Churchill, of a European army? What was Ernest Bevin's longing to 'go down to Victoria Station and buy a ticket to where the 'ell I like'? More to the point, why has it not happened, why can it never happen? And I ask as one who once believed it would. Mr Macmillan, of course, *knows* the answer as well as I do, but because he is of the generation that grew up to the First World War, he cannot *feel* it as those whose earliest conscious memories are of Europe collapsing around them.

Many rough beasts have been born in the past forty years, from inflation to the resurgence of Islam, but none has proved more potent than that search for identity, the nucleus within the atom that can be reduced no further, which we call nationalism.

How can Europe speak with one voice, travel on one passport, buy and sell in one currency, when every now and again Belgians break each other's heads for reasons beyond understanding but clearly based on the belief that some Belgians are more Belgian than others? Or when Spanish Basques murder their fellow-Spaniards to prove that they are not part of Spain? Or when Italians and Austrians come to blows, and sometimes to high explosives, over the spelling of Bolzano? Strange, foreign folk, are they? For answer I do not need to ask you to cross the Irish Sea; would you *literally* stake your life on convincing a roomful of strangers that Monmouth is (or, depending which view you take of the matter, is not) part of Wales?

It has often been observed that no man, however wretched, oppressed, ill, poor or hopeless, would accept from a sorcerer with a magic potion the exchange of his personality and identity with any other man, however affluent and happy the other might be. We would change our *condition* for a different one, or our job, or our house, if by doing so we could better ourselves; we think we would change *ages* with someone younger, though I believe we would jib at the last moment as the potion was being poured; but that which makes us ourselves, and differentiates us from all other selves, we will never give up, whatever the price of keeping it. And so it is with nations.

34

'Tribalism' in Africa has a bad name; any intelligent African who has travelled in Europe must thank his tribal gods that nothing worse than being massacred by a rival tribe is likely to happen to him when he gets home. As I write these words, the West Germans, as loyal Europeans as you could hope to find, are trying to make up their minds whether to bring down a trade war with the United States on the heads of all Europe, in order to encourage their own steel industry; Mrs Thatcher and Mr Peter Walker are working night and day to think of some new insults to level at the agricultural arrangements of our EEC partners; and most of the said partners think we should give the Falkland Islands to Argentina, or, at a pinch, to Brazil.

There are those who think that this state of affairs is deplorable through and through. In its effects, it is; but not in what it says to us about ourselves. Though art transcends nationality – do we think of Mozart as an Austrian or Rembrandt as a Dutchman? – nothing else does, or should. When we stop thinking of ourselves as one nation, we may as well stop thinking of ourselves as fifty-five million individuals: indeed, we shall stop *being* fifty-five million individuals. We have mocked those new African nations who, though they hardly know where their frontiers run, must buy themselves a brand-new national airline the day after independence, to convince themselves, as well as the world, that they exist. The mocking was misplaced, and the Africans wiser than we knew, for man has few higher aims than to feel himself at once a unique and individual soul and part of a definable community of like-minded souls, and that feeling can be induced by a new name on a new aeroplane and indeed new stripes on a new flag. That is why, though Europe may one day decide whether or not to go on paying the Russians to take their surplus butter away, Mr Macmillan, though he is clearly going to live for at least another eighty-eight years, is never going to see his dream realised. Charlemagne can go on sleeping, and Bevin will thump the ticket-office window in vain. Puff out your chests, Britons; why, we even produce the most disgusting football followers in all Europe, as the vomit on the pavements can testify from Oslo to Seville. What can Mr Macmillan's *douceur de vivre* offer to match that?

The Times   October 22nd, 1982

Scarlett runner

The Road to Tara: The Life of Margaret Mitchell
by Anne Edwards*

WHAT DO *War and Peace* and *Gone with the Wind* have in common? Candidates less than fifty years of age should not attempt the question, as they have no chance of getting it right; for that matter, candidates more than fifty-five years old should not attempt it either, as they have no chance of getting it wrong.

These were the two books that the civilians of Britain read in the air-raid shelters, or behind their blacked-out bedroom windows, throughout the Second World War, and both admirably fulfilled the purpose for which they were bought in stupendous numbers. They are very long, so they lasted for months; they are set in the past, which took the readers' minds off the grim present; they are hugely colourful and romantic, which was fitting for a time when colour and romance were in short supply; they contain epic portraits of epic battles, which enabled those in mufti to identify with those who were fighting real epic battles elsewhere; they both hold the attention unflagging throughout their hundreds of thousands of words.

No doubt Tolstoy's is the better book, but its rival for

*Hodder and Stoughton, 1983.

the role of morale-booster to the Home Front did have the qualities I have outlined. And it had an extra advantage; the film of *Gone with the Wind* ran during the war in London (at the little Ritz Cinema, next door to the Empire) for nearly five years, which drove readers to see it and audiences to read the book. It is said that the usherettes eventually knew by heart, word for word, the entire four hours, before presumably being taken off to the funny-farm.

The readers of *War and Peace*, for some of whom it was the first book they had ever read, knew a little about Tolstoy, even if it was no more than that he was a Russian with a big bushy beard. Of the author of *Gone with the Wind*, however, nothing was known except the tittle-tattle, almost all of it untrue, to be found in the film magazines of the day. That in itself was astonishing, for the book had been, and still is, the greatest best-seller in history (the publishers, who had originally decided on a first printing of 10,000, had sold 100,000 before publication, and were to sell more than a million copies in the next six months, 50,000 of them in a single day), but perhaps it was just as well, for the readers of romantic novels like their authors to be romantic, too, and Margaret Mitchell, though there was something of Scarlett (originally called 'Pansy') in her, as there was a good deal of her first, disastrous husband in Rhett Butler, was very far indeed from the flawless porcelain figure the public longed for her to be. For one thing, she drank too much. For another, she was given to unlady-like language and jokes.

No book about her was published before her death; indeed, she screamed blue murder, and threatened litigation, at the mere suggestion of a newspaper 'Profile'. She died (in a car accident she had predicted) in 1949, having left instructions that all her papers should be burned; they were, but her appeal to friends and other correspondents to destroy her letters was ignored by some of them, and gradually enough bits and pieces came to light for a biography. The first one was published in 1965; this is only the second.

Anne Edwards has been exceptionally assiduous in tracking down every scrap of information about the enigmatic author; assiduity, alas, has no effect on a prose style, and hers ('Lieutenant Henry loved to dance as much as Margaret did, and as they floated in each other's arms across the smooth floors of the Capital City Club to the wispy strains of "Poor Butterfly" they were the centre of attention') gave me a vivid idea of what it would be like to be drowned in concentrated bubble-bath liquid.

Margaret Mitchell's horror of publicity, which in any case she could never quite disentangle from a contrary yearning for fame, did not spring from a desire to conceal a shameful past, or at least from a rational desire for such concealment. She was, however, quite hysterical about any mention of her first marriage (not without some justice, as 'Red' Upshaw kept drifting back into her life, and at one point apparently tried to rape her, and may even have succeeded), and hardly less so about the innocent details of her first romantic attachment. The sad truth is that she was clearly a confused and ultimately miserable woman, and could never wholly enjoy or wholly reject her success; though she was constantly dreaming of further literary projects, she never, in the end, wrote another book.

That was not really surprising; Miss Edwards's research emphasises how little Margaret Mitchell's life contained beside her one great triumph. Her tough, suffragette mother was of Huguenot stock, her father of Scottish; her maternal grandmother had been in Atlanta when it was burnt by Sherman. Margaret herself (she never grew beyond five feet) was a tomboy, repeatedly injured in riding accidents; she began to scribble as a child and although she dreamt of qualifying in medicine and becoming a psychiatrist she went – drifted, really – into journalism. She worked for years on *Gone with the Wind* before she would let anybody see it, and even then tried with some success to convince herself that she did not want it published.

It remains her monument. Though it is hardly to be ranked as great literature it is *not* pulp fiction; it paints a wholly credible portrait of the ancient South, romanticised to be sure but not invented, and Margaret Mitchell took limitless pains to get every historical detail correct. But it is more than a daguerreotype; as Miss Edwards says:

> Perhaps the sales of a novel do not determine its literary qualifications, but its lasting images do. And who can now think of the South before, during, and after the Civil War without images drawn from the pages of *Gone with the Wind*?

And perhaps, in one sense, the sales of a novel *do* have some connection with its literary qualifications. The six million people who have bought it in hardback (200,000 copies were sold in Nazi Germany before the war!), were surely not wholly deceived, and surely it will be read when Harold Robbins and Irving Wallace and Frederick Forsyth are forgotten. No work that lasts can be wholly untrue to universal human experience, and any work that has something of universal human experience in it can make out a reasonable claim to be considered art. When the film was being made, Louis B. Mayer was told that it would run for four hours. His reply was 'They'd stone Christ if he came back and spoke for four hours.' For once, the master of giving the public what it wanted was wrong.

Observer July 17th, 1983

Nothing if not critical

THERE IS AN excellent article, written with elegance and passion, in the current *Listener*, by Arnold Wesker; it is a formidable, fair and logically argued presentation of the theatre's case against the critics, and I have never seen it better done, or more worth replying to. Normally, I would not waste five minutes on the theatre's complaints about criticism, particularly the complaints of Mr Wesker, who usually gives the impression that he believes the critics are engaged on a diabolical conspiracy to prevent the truth about his genius from reaching the world. But this time he has drawn up a real indictment, with real arguments, and landed some powerful blows.

His article is very loosely tied to a book of collected criticisms by Mr James Fenton (*You Were Marvellous: Theatre Reviews from the Sunday Times*),★ but he is, rightly, concerned to make a general case, not to find particular fault with Mr Fenton. Before I get to grips with his case, I must summarise it.

'Newspaper reviews', he says, 'render the artist victim of a dangerous deception . . . reviews are merely individual opinions whose importance is magnified out of proportion by print . . . like a teacher's report.

★Cape, 1983.

41

Teachers must always be right, they've been appointed.
The child can only ever be wrong.'

This deception, he argues, is reinforced by a public
attitude which 'regards artistic activity as presumptuous'. Living artists, he says, 'work in a continual state
of original sin from which only a good review can
redeem them . . . The reviewer is St George, print his
sword! The reader, who thrills to a good thrashing, is
on his side before he begins.' Mr Wesker goes on to
instance a woman of his acquaintance who had admired
his work for twenty-five years but did not go to see his
most recent play, *Caritas*, because of the unfavourable
review it had received from Mr Fenton, who 'wrote in
such a way that I felt it wasn't for me'. (To Mr Wesker,
I recommend the reply of de Gaulle when Soustelle
complained that friends were attacking him for support-
ing the General's Algerian policies: '*Changez vos amis.*')

Then Mr Wesker challenges a central claim made by
Mr Fenton, and I think by most critics in one form or
another (certainly I agree with it myself – I was,
incidentally, his predecessor as theatre critic of the
Sunday Times). Mr Fenton demands 'the right to be
wrong, the right to be unfair, the right to be overenthusiastic'. And Mr Wesker asks: 'At whose expense?', and
goes on to say that 'others pay a hidden price' for the
critic's luxury:

A year to write a play, a year before it's produced,
then those unassailable reviews claiming the right to
be unfair. Two years of work wiped out, two years
more to wait . . . Livelihoods, cracked confidence,
pain are involved . . . Mr Fenton must be aware that
he's doing more than simply exercising his right to be
wrong . . . Could he cross his heart and deny that
one tiny part of his ego rubbed its hands together,
smacked its lips and murmured 'That'll make 'em sit
up?'

That, I think, gives a reasonably comprehensive account of Mr Wesker's review of reviewers. Before I get to grips with the substance of it, there are a few lesser matters to get out of the way. Note first that Mr Wesker challenges Mr Fenton's 'right to be wrong, to be unfair'; but though he quotes also the third of Mr Fenton's claims, 'the right to be overenthusiastic', he then falls silent on the subject. Now in the early 1960's, when Mr Wesker was starting in the theatre, with *Roots*, the *Kahn* trilogy and *The Kitchen*, I was hugely and passionately overenthusiastic about Mr Wesker's plays; I had no doubt that his was a real talent, with real depth to it, and I climbed on to the housetops and shouted the news. But I never heard that Mr Wesker was offended by my praise, that he went about saying, 'How dare Levin say that these rough works, in which I'm finding my playwright's feet, are of high quality? Such critics are damaging to the theatre.'

This is not a quibble; the truth is that the theatre demands praise as *its* right, and genuinely believes that favourable reviews are only its due, while unfavourable ones are a kind of treachery. The old Broadway saying 'If you ain't praising 'em, they ain't listening' has a core of literal truth; Mr Wesker claims that the theatre is self-critical, but it is about as self-critical as Louis XIV, and without unfair and wrong-headed critics it would eventually drown in the pool of Narcissus.

Furthermore, Mr Wesker's portrait of the gifted artist, poor-mouthed by the critics, starving in a garret, or even hanging himself from its beams ('Two years of work wiped out . . . cracked confidence, pain . . . '), besides being subject to the same test of even-handedness as the previous point (nobody ever heard a playwright, rejoicing at his new-found prosperity, declaring that the full houses from which he is coining money were filled by the words of the delightful, generous, *supportive* critics), misses a crucial point.

43

What goes on behind the scenes is, in all the senses of the phrase, no business of the critic. His duty is to deal with what comes over the footlights, and whether his review helps to establish or diminish a reputation or an income he is not to concern himself with such matters; that way self-corruption lies.

But there are more important arguments in Mr Wesker's case. His first significant fallacy is his attitude to the influence of the critics. His foolish friend who stayed away was clearly influenced by an adverse review, but I must tell Mr Wesker, difficult though it may be for him to believe it, that Mr Fenton, having written his review, did not go and stand outside the box office with a machine-gun threatening to mow down anyone attempting to buy tickets for the play. And Mr Wesker certainly *won't* believe this, but critics are not Manichees; though they are pleased when patrons buy tickets for plays they have praised, they are not at all upset when the same patrons buy tickets for plays they have excoriated.

Nor will the theatre believe (Mr Wesker says that 'Every time a new, young critic takes over we brace ourselves fearing he is going to flex his muscles on us') that within about three weeks of taking up a critical appointment (during which he lambasts everything that moves) every critic starts to enter theatres on his knees, praying hysterically for something even half-way to tolerable that he can write about. The fact is that almost everything in the theatre is grossly overpraised by the critics, precisely because it is impossible to spend a wholly negative professional life and survive intact. (It was the relentless negativity *in the plays* that finally drove me to leave the reviewer's chair to Mr Fenton.) Mr Wesker will admit, if he is honest (he is), that most of what is put on in the theatre is rubbish without a redeeming feature; but he will make that admission only in general terms, and go on demanding that each particular play is worthy of respect from the critics because it took a long time to write, or because of the playwright's starving wife and nine children.

But there is another sense in which Mr Wesker misunderstands the critics' influence. Reviewing London plays for London audiences, there are about a dozen critics whose views command attention. Very, very rarely indeed do they agree, but let us say that they are unanimous on the striking demerits of play X by playwright Z, and with one accord characterise it as bilge. It closes *instanter*, and Mr Wesker brings in a coroner's verdict of murder by the critics. Is it not more likely that if a dozen people of widely different ages, politics, philosophies, outlooks, tastes, tempers, even sexes, agree that the play was bilge, it actually *was* bilge, and the true verdict should have been suicide by the theatre while of unsound mind?

'Reviewers', says Mr Wesker, 'like to delude themselves that they have a public who trusts them. But did anyone change papers because Fenton took over from Levin?' I've no idea, but the 'delusion' is true, for all that. No individual critic can have an influence on theatre attendances unless his readers have come to feel that he likes the kind of play they like themselves, and dislikes the kind they would wish to avoid; Sir Harold Hobson was a more influential critic on the *Sunday Times* than I was on the *Daily Mail* because a higher proportion of his readers shared his tastes. Mr Wesker, of course, may reply that he is talking only about the critic's influence on art, and that he is indifferent to such commercial considerations as the number of tickets sold; but if he does say that I shall extend my right index finger along the side of my nose, and wink with the other eye.

This argument can never end, but there is a reason for the *perpetuum mobile*. For the last fallacy in Mr Wesker's case is his implicit belief – it runs beneath his whole argument like a subterranean river – that criticism is part of the theatre, and has obligations to it. But criticism is not in any way part of the theatre; for good or ill, it is part of journalism, and always will be. A critic's duty is first to the truth as he sees it ('and it shall follow as the night the day, thou canst not then be false to any man'), second to his readers; but to the theatre, however disgusted and enraged the theatre may be at the fact, not at all.

T.C. Worsley, one of the finest of modern theatre critics, summed it all up when he said that theatre and critic could never be lasting friends, because they worked from different premises, which are embodied in their respective mottoes. The theatre's, he wrote, can be seen in letters of gold above every dressing-room door, and it reads 'Darling, you were wonderful.' But the critic, 'as he dips his ill-paid pen into the ink, looks up at the poker-work motto on his desk, which reads "Don't kid yourself; Keats died of consumption."'

The Times   August 30th, 1983

Journey into genius

Otto Klemperer: His Life and Times Vol.I 1885–1933
by Peter Heyworth★

THE FAMILIAR SUB-TITLE is for once the real clue to a
book; born a Jew in Wilhelmine Germany and thus,
though long since a Catholic convert, forced to flee his
native land on the morrow of Hitler's accession to
power, Klemperer epitomises, more closely than any
other executant musician (or *any* musician other than
Stravinsky), the cultural, political and social history of
central Europe from the fall of Bismarck to the Nazi
Götterdämmerung. This was a man who lived on the
slopes of the Magic Mountain.

As it happens, the second half of his life, though very
different from the first, is in its own way hardly less
evocative of the spirit of the succeeding decades; unfortunately, very few of us are likely to live long enough to
read Mr Heyworth's second and concluding volume, at
any rate unless there is a considerable increase in his
typing-speed, for internal evidence demonstrates that
this instalment has taken him at least nineteen years.

Those who, like me, picked up Klemperer's trail in
the 1950s, think of him – rightly – as the greatest of
classical purists, his performances of Beethoven unsur-

★Cambridge, 1983.

47

passed even by Fürtwängler, of Bach an imperishable monument to the culminating glory of polyphony, of Bruckner responsible for opening our ears to that long-neglected genius. For those who have never learned anything of Klemperer's earlier career, this book will be a revelation.

He was one of the first to revolt against the drudgery and low standards of repertory opera; he was passionately involved in the currents of new music (themselves only part of the turbulent river of new attitudes in all the arts), particularly that of Hindemith, Stravinsky, Weill and Schoenberg; he was strongly influenced by Busoni's theoretical and critical writings; he acquired a reputation for taking up radical positions at a time when radicalism in the arts was inseparable from radicalism in politics – so much so that even had he not been of Jewish origins he would have been marked down by the Nazis as a leading exponent of *Kulturbolschewismus*; above all – it is the glittering pinnacle of this compelling book – his four years at the head of the innovatory and experimental Kroll Opera, though they ended in failure and recrimination (Klemperer himself being no means blameless), sowed seeds that later provided rich, ripe fruit, for neither the 'Bayreuth revolution' ushered in by Wagner's grandsons in 1951 nor the successes of Walter Felsenstein would have taken place if Klemperer had not gone to the Kroll.

All this sounds as though Mr Heyworth's book will be of interest only to those with a passionate love of music and an extensive knowledge of it as well. By no means; it is as remarkable a biography as I have had in my hands for many years, and can be read with immense pleasure by the tone-deaf, provided only that they are capable of being interested in the tormented, passionate life of a man who would still have made his mark on the world if he had been a novelist, a lawyer or indeed a greengrocer.

Throughout Klemperer's London years it was a *secret de Polichinelle* that he was a manic-depressive; Mr Heyworth not only goes into the details of this terrible affliction but traces every swing in it, up and down, throughout Klemperer's life, and shows what it led to each time. Its most notorious effect was his abrupt elopement, in 1912, with the recently married Elisabeth Schumann (I must say that if she looked anything like the picture on page 71 here, St Ignatius Loyola would have run off with her if he had had the chance, never mind the roving-eyed Klemperer), whom he dropped no less abruptly when the manic phase subsided; the affair wrecked his career temporarily, and might well have done so for good.

Another surprise for anyone who remembers the cheers that used to fill the packed Festival Hall after a Klemperer concert is the length of time it took him to become really established even in Germany (his earliest London appearances, in the late 1920s, were largely failures); this was partly due to the excessive caution with which he operated in his depressive phase, but more because of his unprecedented demands for rehearsal-time and control over opera–house standards, and it was this unwavering fidelity to his art that again and again blocked his path. He scarcely knew what 'compromise' meant, but it was not his own vainglory that he sought to enhance, it was the quality of the music he made, which accounts also for much of his appalling behaviour to orchestras and singers, and the appalling rows this led to.

Mr Heyworth's labours have been more than Herculean, his assiduity typified by his tracking down the son of a doctor who ran a nerve clinic to which Klemperer used sometimes to repair for treatment; the doctor died in 1917, but Mr Heyworth was determined to get at the history of Klemperer's visits, and has succeeded in doing so. He has also found and read right through a vast body of documentary evidence, including the dust-laden archives of many a minor opera-house; if it were not for the fact that masses of German material were destroyed by bombing in the Second World War, he would doubtless still be researching.

This mightiest of conductors – only Toscanini dominates his time so completely – served art as passionately as any interpreter of it who ever lived. At the end of his career his twisted, crippled body on the podium symbolised his willingness to go to any lengths, bear any pain, face any foe, to fight his way into the heart of the music and bring its truth to the light. He deserved a fitting memorial, and in this book has got one.

There are a few blemishes; Mr Heyworth is too fond of the 'was to' construction ('He was never to see Mahler again,' 'Klemperer's prophecy . . . was to be all too rapidly fulfilled,' 'Klemperer was never again to conduct *The Ring*'); there are one or two slips in editing – 'generous to a fault' occurs in successive sentences and 'on this occasion' both sides of the clause it is qualifying; he quotes rather too many long-forgotten critics; he makes countless references to Klemperer's enormous height, but never tells us what it actually was; though he is justly severe on Strauss's shamefully time-serving behaviour *vis-à-vis* the Nazis, he is far too indulgent to Tietjen, a kind of musical Hattersley leaping nimbly from bandwagon to bandwagon. But the prodigious mass of facts is marshalled with a steady hand, the footnoting is exemplary, and there is an outstanding index, its compiler – Frederick Smyth – for once acknowledged: *o si sic omnes*.

Mr Heyworth tells Klemperer's heroic and tragic story with a fitting sense of drama and full human understanding and sympathy. It is difficult to see how any musical biography could be done better, and impossible to see how this particular one could.

Observer   October 16th 1983

No smoke . . .

YOU ALL KNOW the story of the Boy Scout troop who were asked what good deed they had done that day, and answered that they had taken an old lady across the road. 'But why', asks the scoutmaster, 'did it need eight of you to do that?' 'Because', comes the reply, 'she didn't want to go.' It is my belief that those eight precocious masters of the art of doing other people good against their will have grown up and are all working in the anti-smoking industry. Moreover, the leader of the patrol, whose uniform was covered with so many proficiency badges he could hardly stand upright, was Mr David Simpson, who is now the director of Action on Smoking and Health, known as ASH (my forthcoming study of the subject, which is the fruit of many years detailed research, will show conclusively that acronyms give you lung cancer), and he hasn't changed a bit.

But this time I think he has Gone Too Far. He was replying, at the weekend, to a comment in the *Sunday Telegraph*, in which the writer had mildly deplored the fanaticism of the anti-smoking industry. Mr Simpson began in characteristic style by claiming that the writer's attitude stemmed from the fact that he is a heavy smoker; it really does seem impossible to get into Mr Simpson's head the fact that some people, regardless of their own habits, find genuinely repellent the desire of him and his kind to make everybody behave as they do themselves, and to harass, insult, intimidate and ultimately use the law against them until they do.

Well, there is one charge Mr Simpson cannot bring against me; my opposition to his fanaticism cannot be based upon my desire to go on smoking, because I don't smoke, and dislike the practice a good deal. I have never been a cigarette smoker; about once a month I used to smoke a cigar, but I doubt if my rate is now more than one a year. So at least I come with clean hands to the fray, and I shall do Mr Simpson the justice of believing that he will not argue that I am in the pay of the tobacco industry, though to judge from the correspondence I get whenever I write about this subject, the same cannot be said about some of his followers.

To the fray, however. The lengths to which the anti-smokers will go is exquisitely demonstrated in another part of Mr Simpson's reply. Defending (as of course I would also) the right of the Duke of Gloucester to be patron of the anti-smoking organisation, he said that

> The duke's keen, active and concerned patronage of ASH reflects the seriousness of our work and responsibilities; and no doubt members of the royal family might wish ASH had been around for much longer, seeing that smoking killed our last four kings.

Our last four kings, as any standard reference book will confirm, were Edward VII, George V, Edward VIII and George VI, and one point must immediately be conceded to Mr Simpson: they are all undoubtedly dead. The matter, however, cannot be allowed to rest there, and it is the reason why it cannot be allowed to rest there that provides the subject of my remarks today.

Edward VII died, in 1910, at the age of sixty-nine, a

span somewhat above average for those days. George V died in 1936 at seventy-one (par for the course), the Duke of Windsor at seventy-eight, well above average, and George VI at fifty-seven, well below it.

All four of these monarchs smoked; the last of them contracted lung cancer, and may be presumed to have died of it. As Mr Simpson knows, but will wriggle himself into sciatica rather than admit, the link between smoking and lung cancer, though undoubtedly very strong, cannot prove that any particular sufferer from the latter got it from the former, and still less can it prove that smoking was the *only* cause. Still, I certainly cannot prove the opposite case, and Mr Simpson is entitled to the *probability* that smoking killed George VI. One down and three to go.

Edward VII suffered from a number of diseases (including lechery, gluttony and gambling, though even Mr Simpson would not claim that these are induced by smoking); he had typhoid in 1871, a form of appendicitis in 1902 and some bronchial trouble in the year of his death, which was very abrupt. There is no evidence from which we may conclude that he was 'killed by smoking', and precious little that his smoking had anything to do with his final illness.

George V played golf, gave up drinking throughout the First World War (if it comes to that, George VI gave up *smoking* throughout the Second) and broke his pelvis in a riding accident in 1915, but he survived all these catastrophes without lasting harm. He also survived, though much more narrowly, a streptococcal infection picked up in 1928; that was eight years before his death, and he made a complete recovery from it. In his case, there is not the slightest reason to suppose that smoking ever did him any harm at all.

Edward VIII enjoyed generally good health throughout his very long life; he was a fairly silly man most of the time, but again, Mr Simpson would presumably not argue that smoking causes softening of the brain. As for the present Queen, she doesn't smoke at all, and anyway is still alive, so *that's* all right.

Now estimate, to three places of decimals, the degree of self-deceptive intolerance from which a man must suffer to take the above facts and turn them into 'smoking killed our last four kings'. Having done that exercise, try working out how far you would trust the same man to tell you the time of day and get it right in fewer than three goes. It is not too much to say that Mr Simpson and his kind are firmly convinced, or at any rate behave as though they are convinced, that if any person first smokes and then dies, it must follow as the night the day that the smoking was the direct and sole cause of the dying. It is useless for me to tell Mr Simpson that my maternal grandfather smoked fifty cigarettes a day throughout his adult life (his last breath was used, literally, to inhale his last puff) and died at the age of eighty-four, because he will undoubtedly reply that if grandpa hadn't smoked he would have lived to 168, and I cannot prove him wrong. But I can prove him reckless and absurd in his fanaticism, and on the whole I think I just have.

Smoking is undoubtedly dangerous; nobody should be encouraged to do it, or to admire it. It is also a fairly nasty habit. It undoubtedly aggravates many illnesses, and no less undoubtedly causes some of them, and fatalities therefrom. But no one can say that *this* man contracted lung cancer and died of it *because* he smoked, whether the corpse was of a king or a ratcatcher, and it is worth adding that some people contract lung cancer without ever setting eyes on a cigarette. And to claim that 'smoking killed our last four kings' is not merely nonsense; it is the thirteenth chime of the clock, which casts doubt on all that has gone before, and diminishes the effect of Mr Simpson's more sensible work.

It is well that there are organisations which seek to

draw our attention to the dangers of smoking, but it is not at all well that the members of such organisations should behave as though smokers are *hostes humani generis*, or as though the rules of evidence do not apply to those who campaign to stop them smoking. Those of you who have German may take extra comfort from the following verse; it is impossible to translate gracefully, but I offer a very free version to my monoglot readers:

> *Alkohol und Nikotin*
> *Rafft die halbe Menschheit hin;*
> *Ohne Alkohol und Rauch,*
> *Stirbt die andere Hälfte auch.*

If you smoke and if you drink,
It is later than you think;
If such poison's not your game,
You will perish just the same.

The Times   December 22nd, 1983

. . . without fire

I HAVE TO return today to the subject of smoking; more precisely, of the campaign against smoking. I do not much relish taking the part of those who do something unpleasant and risk-beset that I do not, and would not, do myself, but the anti-smoking industry has ensured that it is almost impossible for a smoker to defend smoking without having his motives impugned by the industry's spokesmen, so as a non-smoker willing to defend the smoker's rights, however deplorable his habits, I find myself conscripted in the cause, and dragged on to the battlefield over my insistence that I am a non-combatant and from a neutral country.

The latest round began when Mr David Simpson, head of the anti-smoking industry as director of ASH (Action on Smoking and Health), and most zealous of all the fanatics active on his side of the argument, declared, without qualification, that 'Smoking killed our last four kings'.

I greeted this preposterous claim with thumb to nose; it is preposterous because no one can say that any particular person died because he or she smoked. Smoking is not itself a disease, and the diseases that smokers die from existed before tobacco did, and will continue to exist when Mr Simpson and his unlovely cohorts have made all smoking illegal. Moreover, there is precious little evidence that smoking even helped to kill George V or Edward VIII, and not much that it contributed to the death of Edward VII; only in the case of George VI, who was a heavy smoker and died of lung cancer at an age well below average expectations, can the finger be pointed with any real likelihood that it is pointing in the right direction.

The whole silly story of the royal massacre was started in 1977 in a colour-supplement feature by Mr Oliver Gillie, then as now the medical correspondent of the *Sunday Times*, and a notable practitioner of phobotherapy, or frightening people for their own good; it was he, fittingly enough therefore, who replied to my comments on the subject. But the words in which he did so seem to me to bear out in so striking a manner what I had been saying about the anti-smoking industry and its lack of logic that I feel obliged to examine his reply today.

Mr Gillie claims that he 'revealed' the truth about the death of the four monarchs; as we shall see, all he did was to reveal that they were dead, a discovery that many had made before him. But note, before we go any further, the words he chose to describe his revelation; our last four kings, he said, 'died of smoking diseases'.

Now this is already a fairly far cry from Mr Simpson's 'Smoking killed our last four kings'. For what *is* a 'smoking disease'? Is it a disease that only smokers get? No; all the diseases and afflictions that he attributes to the four dead kings are also suffered by large numbers of people who never smoke at all. Is it then a disease that smokers die from but non-smokers survive? No, there are dead and living in both categories. Well, perhaps it is a disease which you *may* get if you don't smoke, but *invariably* get if you do? No, there are no such diseases. The truth is that a 'smoking disease' is a disease which is contracted by a higher proportion of smokers – a slightly higher proportion in the case of some diseases, a very much higher proportion for other diseases – than non-smokers. But that is much less dramatic than saying 'our last four kings died of smoking diseases', let alone 'smoking killed our last four kings'.

These claims – 'Smoking killed our last four kings', 'our last four kings died of smoking diseases' – are what the French would call, if they used such language, *les mots de belette*, the German for which is *Wieselwörter*. And Mr Gillie has a few more of them up his sleeve, as when he says that the various diseases suffered by the kings 'are all common consequences of smoking'. So they are; they are also the not altogether *un*common consequences of something else – something so extremely else, in fact, that it afflicts people who never smoke at all.

It is generally agreed, by experts much more learned and knowledgeable than Mr Gillie, Mr Simpson and myself, that there is a direct link between smoking and certain diseases or unpleasant medical conditions. Obviously, I do not deny that claim. Obviously, I agree that smoking is dangerous to life or health. Obviously (after all, I do not smoke myself) I do not recommend the practice, and if someone – one of my godchildren, say – were to ask my advice on the matter, I would make a passionate and, I flatter myself, eloquent, case for never touching cigarettes. But three things, when I contemplate the anti-smoking industry, stick in my craw.

The least important of the three is the twisted argument that it leads anti-smokers into; Mr Gillie added, for instance, that 'if they had not smoked and had died of old age these kings might reasonably have expected to live into their eighties', to which I am inclined to say that if they had never been born they wouldn't have died of anything and that if we had some eggs we could have some ham and eggs if we had some ham, or even that if my grandmother had wheels she might well be a bicycle.

The second, worse, trait of the anti-smoking propagandists is their intolerant fanaticism. The language they use about smokers is the language of hate; to call it totalitarian would be very little of an exaggeration, and will soon be none at all. Nor are they content to ensure – and a very reasonable claim it would be – that as far as is possible, public places should have non-smoking as well as smoking sections, as trains and planes and buses already do, along with many restaurants, cinemas and theatres and other institutions patronised by both categories of customer. No; they insist that smoking must be stamped out by law, that public places shall be entirely and exclusively given over to non-smokers, that more and more penalties, burdens and controls should be placed on those who make, advertise or sell cigarettes.

But the third and worst failing of the full-time anti-smokers is their inability to see, or if they see to admit, that what they are advocating is an assault, and in some ways a serious assault, on the individual's freedom to lead his or her own life in whatever directions, including dangerous ones, he or she chooses. The weasel-worded reply to that – I have been getting it in letters by the waggon-load since my last column on the subject – is that the smoker is limiting the freedom of others not to smell smoke. No one who can put forward that argument as of equal weight with the real argument over freedom is likely to be clear enough in mind to understand the fallacy, but I might as well point it out anyway. To choose whether we smoke is part of a great *right* – the greatest really – the right to govern our own lives, and not to have others govern them for us. But the experience of being in a smoky atmosphere is a *nuisance*. If you really cannot tell the difference, I do not wish to hear from you.

All societies whose leaders have tried to make the citizens good by compulsion have come to grief, and the grief has almost invariably been that of the citizens, not the leaders. What is more, men have sometimes followed will-o'-the-wisps into swamps, and drowned, heedless of warning signs, notices in the local newspapers, the advice of the landlord at the inn, or the annual statistics of swamp fatalities and their significant correlation with the incidence of will-o'-the-wisps. There is another way of reducing such deaths; it is to station men all round the swamps, carrying chains and armed with legal powers to fasten them firmly round the wrists and ankles of the reckless traveller. I have a nasty feeling that when ASH has eliminated all smoking by law its leading members will begin to express concern about the dangers lurking in swamps.

The Times January 20th, 1984

Venice preserved

THERE WAS I, in the Royal Academy, standing in front of Titian's 'The Flaying of Marsyas' and doing no harm to anybody, when up comes Professor John Hale himself and seizes my arm. 'By thy long grey beard and glittering eye', I enquired, 'now wherefore stopp'st thou me?' He held me with his glittering eye (I could not choose but hear), and thus spake on that ancient man, the bright-eyed Mariner. 'You must write', he said, 'an entire article about this picture.' I demurred, but thought it only right to give my reasons. 'I fear thee, ancient Mariner,' I remarked; 'I fear thy skinny hand. And', I added, 'thou art long, and lank, and brown, as is the ribbed sea-sand.'

Eftsoons his hand dropt he. But as a matter of fact, though I am unable to respond to very late Titian, the picture is practically the only item in this gigantic and sumptuous array of masterpieces that I could *not* write an entire article about, and the first thing I must do, therefore, is to salute, with admiration, amazement, gratitude and reverence, Professor Hale and the team he has led in devising and putting together *The Genius of Venice 1500–1600*, surely the mightiest show to grace the walls of the academy in living memory.

It starts, as well it might, with the Barbari map of Venice, and goes on with Carpaccio's 'Lion of St Mark',

61

ripped from the walls of the Doge's Palace to delight Londoners. Then, after an account of the second Battle of Lepanto (one of the reasons, dear reader, why you and I are not Mohammedans), the visitor turns right, through an archway.

Pause in that opening. It is the first of a series, all in line; look, therefore, straight across the long gallery that lies before you, across the next room and the next. The eye fetches up against the far wall of the last gallery in the series. There, dead ahead of you but forty yards away, is a Lorenzo Lotto, of St Christopher with the Christ-child, that you simply will not believe possible. Ignore the riches to right and left – there is plenty of time – and march straight towards the Lotto, convinced that as you get closer it will prove to be a striking but ordinary picture. You will find that, on the contrary, your first impression from a distance conveyed no more than a hint of the roaring furnace of energy and colour that the canvas holds. (The catalogue note, by Professor Pietro Zampetti, says demurely that the painting is 'of great chromatic intensity'.)

Retrace your steps. Enter the first gallery you looked across to see the Lotto. It is *bulging* with Titians; the exhibition includes twenty of his paintings, together with eight drawings. Leave out the 'Marsyas', on which we shall never agree, and come and stand with me before the 'Portait of Ranuccio Farnese'; without moving your feet you can see also his 'Portrait of Two Boys' and his 'Tarquin and Lucretia' (another late picture, but without the dangerously free draughtsmanship that makes me uneasy in the 'Marsyas'); no great distance away is his 'Portrait of Cristofero Madruzzo'. These people cry out with the life in them; not Rembrandt himself, born twenty years after Titian died, set the blood pulsing more strongly through his figures, and the virility in Titian is a quality shared by almost all these Venetians.

Tintoretto is represented almost as amply as Titian; so is Veronese, on whom I dote more than any of the other artists of Venice (would that it had been possible to remove the end wall of Gallery X from the Accademia and bring it here to show us his 'Supper at the House of Levi', all forty-two feet of it); Lotto, Moroni, Bassano, Paris Bordone, Palma Vecchio, Pordenone – all these artists are strewn about the Royal Academy until next March as though the lenders didn't love them, which in the case of the Accademia often seems to be true.

There is no painting by Carpaccio other than the 'Lion', but there are three drawings, and one of them will make every Carpaccio-lover, and indeed every Venice-lover, howl with the yearning to go at once to the Scuola di S. Giorgio degli Schiavoni, for it is a sketch of what became the last picture in the St Jerome series there, little white dog and all.

I could go on for hours picking plums out of the pie, but this exhibition is not just a collection of masterpieces; it is the gorgeous sun-face of Venice in the days of her swelling pride and assured achievement. The century had begun in defeat; the coalition of Italian states, angered and frightened by the apparently irresistible growth of Venetian power, had allied themselves with the Turks, who destroyed a Venetian fleet at the first Battle of Lepanto in 1499 and imposed humiliating terms on the arrogant republic.

The sixteenth century is the story of how Venice regained her former position; seventy-two years after the first Lepanto, she had her revenge at the second:

Cervantes on his galley sets the sword back in the
    sheath
(Don John of Austria rides homeward with a wreath.)
And he sees across a weary land a straggling road in
    Spain,

Up which a lean and foolish knight forever rides in
vain,
And he smiles, but not as Sultans smile, and settles
back the blade . . .
(But Don John of Austria rides home from the Crusade.)

Long before the century's close, of course, the seeds
of decay had begun to sprout; by the end of the
seventeenth century Venice was worm-eaten through
and through, and it was an empty shell that Napoleon
blew down with a single breath. Let us be thankful that
nobody concerned in this exhibition wanted to take it to
the middle of the eighteenth century, so that we would
have seen Canaletto and Tiepolo fiddling while Venice
burned.

We see the work of some of the most confident artists
in all history, painting, living and working in a polity
that had not yet lost its overweening confidence in its
own power, riches and endurance. They were not, the
geniuses who adorn the Academy, court painters in any
sense; they had to watch their step, of course, and
Veronese got into frightful trouble with the Inquisition
for 'Supper at the House of Levi' itself, being accused of
blasphemy for the wonderful informality of it all. And
an artist painting a great nobleman of the city would not
have put the warts in even if the sitter had asked him to.
But no one can go to *The Genius of Venice* and fail to
realise that these men knew their own quality, and
thought it no shame to demonstrate what they knew. If
you doubt me, go back and take another look at the
Lotto 'St Christopher'.

The exhibition is vast, but I would have liked it
vaster; I would like to have seen more of the *objets* –
glass, jewellery, furniture – of sixteenth-century
Venice. (There are some fine sculptures, most of them
small, which hint at what we are missing. But this is
greed on my part, as is my feeling that invisible

64

orchestras should be gently playing Monteverdi as we go round.) What we have is magnificent, for it is a demonstration of a century of art that makes a statement as clear, assertive and unambiguous about its time and place as does the voice of Renaissance Florence, or for that matter the Funeral Oration of Pericles and Shakespeare's *Histories*. (The catalogue, in scope and quality, is fully worthy of what it records.)

On the whole, the artists of sixteenth-century Venice did not paint their own history or their own time, apart from what can be read from their portraits; Carpaccio's 'Lion' was the republic's sign-manual, it is true, but he is in heaven at this moment for the St Jeromes and the St Ursulas. All the same, it is history, and not just art history, that floods Burlington House, and from the moment we see the Barbari at the entrance we are part of another world, another time, and we remain conscious of that otherness through every step we take. It is said that the Royal Academy has gambled heavily on this exhibition, which can either restore its fortunes, or bring it close to disaster, according to whether it is a success or a failure. It deserves to be the greatest success in the Academy's history; as for Professor Hale, the Academicians should make him a present of the Michelangelo *tondo* to put on his mantelpiece.

The Times   December 3rd, 1983

The saved and the just

The Last Jews in Berlin by Leonard Gross*

OF ALL THE by-products of the Holocaust, the story told in this book is perhaps the strangest and most pitiful. It concerns those German Jews who, from the beginning of Nazi rule to the end of the war and from the first disabilities heaped upon their people in the nascent Reich to the days of the Final Solution as the Gestapo roamed the streets looking for survivors to ship to Auschwitz, lived in hiding and, against fearful odds, survived.

Some lived rough; some got out of the country through the heroic efforts of Swedish churchmen posted to wartime Germany; some, including the handful whose stories Mr Gross has chosen to tell in this book as representative, were hidden by courageous and honourable German Gentiles who risked their own lives to abide by Portia's rule:

> Though justice be thy plea, consider this,
> That in the course of justice none of us
> Should see salvation: we do pray for mercy,
> And that same prayer doth teach us all to render
> The deeds of mercy.

*Sidgwick and Jackson, 1983.

One by one, as the terror closed in, Mr Gross's band of survivors, the 'U-boats', as such Jews called themselves (like U-boats they lived beneath the surface but had to take the risk of coming up from time to time), found refuge. The providers of the refuge were even more varied than the Jews they hid; from a blonde Aryan society beauty who was already working in the Resistance to a couple who were at first deeply reluctant to have anything to do with the Jews who sought their help, they shrugged and rose to giant human stature.

Much of the material in the survivors' accounts reads like the most lurid fiction, but the author, though this is a reporter's study rather than a scholar's, has checked everything that can be checked, and questioned both sheep and shepherds carefully; there can be no doubt that these stories are true not only in outline but in detail, including even the two cases of 'U-boats' who were betrayed and caught by the Gestapo but who managed to escape while waiting for the transports that were to take them to extermination, and to take up their underground life again where they had left off.

That word 'betrayed' covers the most terrible of all the darknesses in this book. There were Jews working for the Nazis as 'catchers'; they would prowl round areas where they knew Jews had formerly lived, or where they suspected they were being given refuge; if they spotted any of the U-boats coming up for air (and sometimes the refugees had not dared to venture out of doors for months on end) they would turn them in, sometimes using abominable trickery, to their enemies. We even know the names of two of them: Rolf Isaaksohn and Stella Kübler, and the latter, who served ten years in prison for her crimes, is still living in Berlin.

Some of the survivors, like the highly intellectual Hans Hirschel or the forceful and commanding Fritz Croner, had great inner resources that helped them to survive, but it is not as simple as that, for Willy Glaser had no such strength to fall back on; the only thing he knew was that he was irremediably mediocre (when he went underground he had no money, no papers and no idea what to do), yet he, too, came through.

None of them would have survived for a week, of course, if it had not been for their benefactors, some of whom took horrifying risks to keep the hunted victims safe. For they needed not just hiding-places but food and identity-papers (which were necessary to obtain ration-cards), together with leak-proof stories for the neighbours to explain a strange face behind the curtains. The protectors' attitude was summed up by Joseph Wirkus, one of those who were at first unwilling to get involved, protesting that the refugees could only stay briefly, and ended by not only hiding them for years but by adding other refugees until the house was bursting with them: at each step that led inevitably to another and more dangerous step, Wirkus would intone 'We have said A, now we must say B,' and marched stolidly on down his logical and heroically generous path.

Perhaps even more remarkable was the action of many of the shepherds' neighbours; it eventually transpired that almost all the sheepfolds were surrounded by people who knew perfectly well what was going on, but who, though they did not dare to go so far as to shelter refugees themselves, never betrayed them. There was even a Gestapo officer who, in the course of an interrogation and under the nose of his brother-interrogator, managed to drop a life-saving hint.

This book tells the story of those who were not caught; those who were (and whose benefactors must have died with them) were not in a position to answer the author's questions. Estimates vary of the numbers of Jews who survived in the capital of a regime sworn to kill them; perhaps a few thousand, perhaps only a few hundred. Mr Gross's group remained in Berlin after the war ended and made new lives for themselves; two of the men married their shepherdesses; perhaps even Willy Glaser was not as mediocre as he thought.

The book is another nail in the coffin of the Manichee; the reader takes from it a vivid and enduring memory of goodness on the part of the saviours while the evil of the persecutors, though omnipresent, remains the backdrop to the drama. Truly, death shall have no dominion; Abraham's plea that the Lord should spare the cities of the plain if fifty righteous men should be found there would certainly have served to save Berlin.

Observer   August 7th, 1983

Let us now praise famous men

THERE ARE BARGAINS galore to be had in Pyongyang, and if you think that that is a long way to go even for bargains, know that these can be obtained without your needing to stir from your hearth, merely by sending payment in advance through the Bank of China office in London. (French bargain-hunters should apply to the Banque Française du Commerce Extérieur. The commercially minded in West Germany and Switzerland are also catered for, and I will gladly supply the details of the banks to which they should apply, on receipt of an international reply coupon. Trade discount is offered for orders in quantity.)

Before you all hock the candlesticks and devise precautions to avoid being trampled to death in the rush, I must reveal that the bargains available do not include no-questions-asked gold bullion, or even transistor radios. They consist almost entirely of the thoughts of KIM IL SUNG, dictator of North Korea since 1948, and I have a catalogue of the lot, published by the Korea Publications Export and Import Corporation, to prove it.

We kick off with a volume bearing the catchy title *Works*; it includes 'speeches, reports, conclusions, talks, articles, etc.', and contains 480 pages. It will set you back a mere £1.70, but if you think that is a snip, just wait; the very next entry in the catalogue, which has an even sexier title (*On the Building of the Workers' Party of Korea*) and a real come-on for a blurb – 'The book carries the works of the great leader President KIM IL SUNG which give all-round answers to the principled (*sic*) problems associated with building, strengthening and developing the Workers' Party of Korea' – is, at £1.20 for 686 pages, practically being given away, notwithstanding that for reasons unexplained it is available only in German.

At this point I suspect that the blurb-writer was taken away and shot for being insufficiently enthusiastic, a charge that certainly cannot be levelled against his successor, for the next volume (450 pages for £1.25) 'contains the immortal works of the great leader KIM IL SUNG on the historical necessity of the three revolutions', and the one after offers, at the same length and price, 'the immortal classics' of the said great leader, swiftly followed (200 pp., £0.70) by 'the immortal classics of the great leader KIM IL SUNG giving comprehensive answers to the complex theoretical and practical problems arising from the complete materialization of the socialist rural question in our country'; I can hardly wait for the film, particularly if they keep the title: *For the Complete Materialization of the Theses of the Rural Question.*

So it goes on, from 'Propositions advanced by the great leader President KIM IL SUNG on the essence and principle of intellectualization of the whole society' to 'the unique idea and policy of the great leader President KIM IL SUNG on the socialist transformation of private trade and industry', and from 'the writings of the great leader President KIM IL SUNG about the historical necessity of agricultural cooperation' to 'a systematization of the perfect answers of the great leader' (guess who), after which it does not seem surprising to come upon a *Brief History of the Revolutionary Activities of the Great*

Leader Comrade KIM IL SUNG which 'gives a brief description of the immortal, glorious revolutionary activities of the great leader of our people'. (Views on brevity doubtless differ; this book is 352 pages brief. Mind you, it only costs a quid.)

And that is merely the current publication catalogue; when we get to the back-list we find the complete works of thingummy in 10 volumes, which will cost you a laughable £16.85 for 5,204 variously glorious, heroic and perfect pages.

There is a good deal more of this stuff, including a Short Biography of our hero in two volumes totalling 900 pages, and even a novel dealing with 'the brilliant revolutionary activities conducted by the great leader President KIM IL SUNG in the first half of 1936' (no doubt the sequel will deal with the no less brilliant revolutionary activities of our leader in the *second* half of 1936), but I think I have provided as much information as even the most cautious potential customer could want before forking out.

Having thus done my duty by commerce, I think I am entitled to a more general reflection or two. Haven't *any* of the more horrible rulers of this world's ample supply of totalitarian states ever heard of Ozymandias? Evidently not, and the most sobering aspect of that sufficiently sobering truth is that this kind of lunacy is not confined to the Amins and Castros and Bokassas and KIM IL SUNGS; at one time, in China, there were *seven hundred million* pictures of Mao Tse Tung in circulation, and not long before he died Brezhnev awarded himself the Lenin Prize *for literature.*

The worms got Mao, and having finished him turned to Brezhnev. They will get Kim Il Sung too, and eventually even 'the dear Comrade Kim Jong Il, the sole successor to the great leader President Kim Il Sung and sugacious (*sic*) leader of our Party and people'; what shall it profit a man if he gain forty yards of library shelving and lose his own eyeballs?

I'm damned if I know. Lord Beaverbrook used to arrange for favourable articles about him to be published in his newspapers, thus making him the only conjuror ever to evince surprise at finding a white rabbit in his top-hat, but he was notoriously afraid of hell-fire, and the concept of hell-fire would no doubt be dismissed as bourgeois sentimentality by Kim Il Sung and his like.

But what if, behind that confident dismissal, a very old Adam is lurking? I do not really suppose that many of these mad brutes come to believe, even *in articulo mortis*, that they are going to a judgement which not all their sycophants can help them evade, but there is a lesser form of doubt which may well trouble them sufficiently to explain their insatiable hunger for being praised by people they have hired for the sole purpose of praising them.

Perhaps, you see, they have heard of Ozymandias after all, and even of Dorian Gray. Perhaps, clearly audible above the cheering they have ordered, there is a still, small voice which insists on telling them the terrible truth, which is that they are nothing, their rule is nothing, their Collected Works are nothing, the reverence of their subjects is nothing, the banners, the medals, the sashes, the music, even the power – no, *especially* the power – all these are nothing, and that five minutes after they die it will be as though they had never been born.

Imagine murdering your way to the top of the society you live in, only to discover first that what you are standing on is only a dungheap and second that, even if you commission a statue of yourself five miles high, your political achievements, like the writings to which dutiful hacks obediently put your name, will not rate more than a footnote in the history books, even the ones published by your 'dear comrade and sole successor', who will in any case be too busy having his own Collected Works written and praised.

The pain of such a *memento mori* can only be assuaged, evidently, by more of the same medicine; if the publication of ten volumes of collected rubbish will not shut out the fear of mortality, publish twenty, and if one portrait is not sufficiently flattering, try 700 million. For that matter, if the killing of one enemy of the people does not bring dreamless sleep, kill thousands, and if they will not suffice, say it in millions. Yet I will wager that the still, small voice will continue to be heard, crying 'Sleep no more!' to all the house.

If I am right, it must be good news; in a sense, the best news ever told. For it means that one tiny truth is more powerful than a million great lies, that a buffoon and scoundrel, though his name is spelt in capital letters, is still only a buffoon and scoundrel, that the eternal sieve of the universe, which shakes through the dross, is still in good working order. When Kim Il Sung has finished his Collected Works, let him try the Collected Works of Montaigne, where he will find the last word on the subject: 'Sit we on never so high a stool, we sit but upon our own tails.'

The Times June 27th, 1983

Relative values

THEY ORDER THIS matter better in Copeland; or if not
better, then without doubt differently. Copeland is
in Cumbria, and not so long ago, it seems, the local
council sent to ask those of its tenants who were behind
with the rent why this was so; the problem was a
pressing one, apparently, because nearly half of all those
dwelling in municipal property in the area were in
arrears, and the resultant hole in the municipal books
had had to be filled up, come ratepaying time, by the
other half.

Only two of the answers given on the doorstep to the
man in the bowler hat were published; in those two
replies, however, there rests much matter for wonder.
One family (the breadwinner was earning some £7,500 a
year) said that they could not afford to pay the rent
because they were already paying £25 a week for the
hire of five television sets and three video recorders.
Another family in the area had got behind with the rent
because of the cost of a summer holiday they had taken
in Algeria; when the collector ventured the opinion that
that must have set them back a bob or two, they
explained that the Algerian trip had been necessary
because although they had already had one holiday that
year in Malta, it had rained while they were there. The
council (Labour-controlled, incidentally) thereupon

took steps to regain possession of the rent-owing families' houses.

No doubt the news of this oppressive and unjust action will shortly lead to a series of denunciatory articles in *New Society,* and to indignant questions in Parliament by Mr Jack Straw. No doubt, too, shortly I shall receive letters accusing me of wanting to send women down the mines and induce rickets in children. None the less, I wish to discuss the implications of the tale, twirling my villain's moustache as I do so.

Somewhere in the heads of the tenants in question there is firmly lodged the belief that it is not necessary for people today to deny themselves anything in the way of comfort or material possessions in order to meet their financial obligations, together with the equally powerful conviction that when those obligations are in respect of necessities and/or owed not to an individual but to an institution – a credit-card organisation, a shop, a mail-order company, the local council – there is no reason for disquiet, let alone shame, in their debts or in the reason for the debts being incurred.

I cannot agree, but that is of no importance. What is important is to discover how those ideas got into those heads in the first place. When Mr Alex Lyon said in the House of Commons that the state – he meant in this country, not in totalitarian lands – should be responsible for all the necessities of life for all its citizens, leaving the citizens free to spend the entire fruits of their earned incomes on indulging their tastes in leisure or luxury, he was speaking the epilogue, not writing the preface; the idea had clearly taken root long before. Indeed, the roots must already have gone deep, for the only voice raised to express surprise at the view was that of my colleague Ronald Butt, and it is well known that *he* wants to send little boys up chimneys and make membership of a trade union punishable by transportation for life.

Somehow it has come to be felt that when St Paul said to the Thessalonians that 'if any man would not work, neither should he eat', St Paul was wrong, and that when he said in his Third Epistle to the same people (who had ignored the first two) 'if any man would not pay his rent, neither should he hire five television sets and three video recorders', he was not only wrong but plainly barmy.

The trouble began, I think, in the use of the word 'poverty', and the reason it caused trouble lay in the fact that it cannot be defined except in relative terms. An unemployed and partly disabled elderly woman living in one room of a condemned tenement in the Gorbals would, I think, be held to be poor by any reader of these words. But to a family living on the pavement in Calcutta the Gorbals woman is a Maharanee dwelling in fabulous luxury. So much is obvious (though you would be surprised at how widely it is not understood); what is less obvious is that the usual answer to the point implied in the comparison – that the Gorbals woman does not live in India but in a country where most people live in decent houses or flats – won't do either. For what, under the new dispensation, does the Gorbals woman need to be no longer poor?

Certainly she needs the leaky roof mended; she needs more and better food; she needs heat, clothes, washing facilities. But that is what she needs to avoid break-down, starvation or hypothermia; what does she need to be no longer thought of as poor? It may be difficult to believe, but there is no possible answer to that question.

In 1982 the proportion of households in Britain with a television set was 97 per cent; were the other 3 per cent poor? It seems they must have been, for to lack what almost everybody else has is the accepted definition of poverty. Then a television set is a necessity. But wait: the 97 per cent of households with a television set were divided into 77 per cent with a colour set and 20 per cent

with a black and white. Not to have what three-quarters
of the population do have must be to live in poverty;
then a colour set is a necessity. Is that not an odd
conclusion?

You can go on playing this game all night; but the
point is that we have been playing it nationally for
years, and the referees have been – still are – such folk as
Professor Peter Townsend and Mr Frank Field. There is
no level of income whatever that cannot be thought to
constitute poverty if a substantial proportion of other
incomes are larger, and the number of items that, year
by year, are struck off the luxury list and added to the
necessities category never diminishes, nor can it ever
diminish, until we reach Mr Lyon's Nirvana and everything it is possible to desire has become essential.

And all the families in Copeland were doing was to
get very slightly ahead of the game. Indeed, the second
family was hardly even that; most people have holidays,
so surely only the poverty-stricken do not, and if it be
said that most people do not have holidays in Algeria to
make up for the rain that fell on their holidays in Malta,
I can promise that it will not be said much longer.

For the rent-dodgers in Copeland television sets,
video recorders and two foreign holidays a year constitute a *right*, an *entitlement*, whereas the rent represents a
duty, an *obligation*. For decades, without cease, we have
been daily and hourly fashioning new rights and entitle-
ments, and abolishing old duties and obligations, until
the idea that anyone has a duty and an obligation to be
television-poor, video-poor, abroad-poor (let alone
drink-poor and cigarette-poor) until he has paid the
rent, and no right or entitlement to these things until he
has settled the grocer's bill, will seem, and not only to
Messrs Lyon, Townsend and Field, to be the most
outlandish and laughable idea ever proposed in the
columns of a serious newspaper.

It is no use my saying that once upon a time that was

not so, for I shall merely be told that once upon a time we burnt old women for witches, and now we know better. But until the broken connexion is restored, until we see again that credit and debit must balance, that rights must be derived from something more than wants and duties may not be ignored without penalty, that it is not necessary to have five television sets, three video-recorders and two Mediterranean holidays a year and that even if it were it would still be necessary to pay the rent first – until then, we shall continue, as a nation, to slither down the spiral, and the rent-collector in Copeland will ply the knocker in vain.

The Times January 6th, 1983

The reluctant mole

After Long Silence by Michael Straight*

THIS UNPLEASANT BOOK, written in the prose of a
Hollywood press-agent and oozing implausibility
from every page, is the autobiography of a man who
was intimately involved with a pre-war Cambridge
circle which became part of a wider group in Britain and
the United States working on behalf of the Soviet
Union, and, where they had the opportunity, betraying
their countries in the Soviet interest.

Mr Straight confesses that, after he had been re-
cruited, he gave various documents to a Russian
appointed as his 'control', but denies that he gave, or
indeed had, or sought access to, any secret material; he
further claims that even if he had been in a position to
pass classified information, he would never have done
so. He knew from the start or near it that such men as
Blunt, Long and Burgess were full-fledged spies, but he
kept the knowledge to himself long after the date at
which he claims to have broken entirely with communism, let alone the Soviet Union; indeed, he remained
silent for twenty-six years and finally spoke only when,
offered an American Government job by President

*Collins, 1983.

Kennedy (as Chairman of the National Endowment for the Arts), he discovered that this would mean a thorough 'positive vetting'.

I do not like thee, Dr Fell. In the first place, the book is full of conversations, supposedly recalled *verbatim* and printed in quotation marks, dating back years or even decades. I am myself blessed with a freak memory, which can recover incidents and remarks from a similar distance, but I would never claim to be able to remember dialogue in that fashion, especially when, as in this book, some of the conversations could not have seemed important at the time, taking on significance only years later.

In the second place, Mr Straight seems less concerned to tell us how he became a parlour-Stalinist, and what it led him to do and refrain from doing for the next quarter of a century, than to paint himself as a kind of revolving hero (that is, a hero whichever way you look at him, on the analogy of Harry Truman's definition of a revolving sonofabitch). Thus, he is a social hero as an undergraduate, ashamed of his wealth and privileges, a communist hero in the 1930s, passionate to stop Hitler, a radical hero in the 1940s, warning Henry Wallace against communist infiltration, a liberal hero in the 1950s, condemning McCarthyism, a patriotic hero in the 1960s, shopping his friends at last, and a concerned-democrat hero now, weighing the dangers of the international situation with a world-weary shrewdness; by the time he has finished, it is difficult not to feel that he thinks he deserves a separate medal for each of his heroisms, and a special commendation for being less helpful to the Soviet Union than he might have been. Professor Anthony Blunt claimed to have been faced with the choice of 'betraying my country or betraying my friends', and there is a great deal of the same kind of cant in this book.

In the third place, there is what might be called the

book's ring of inauthenticity, exemplified in his account of what he says was his last meeting with his Soviet control, a man whom he says he knew only as 'Michael Green': 'I handed one last memorandum to Green. It was a plea to the Soviet Government to give up its revolutionary ideology in the interests of world peace.' No doubt the fault is in me, but I find myself quite unable to believe that, or for that matter this:

> On three occasions between 1949 and 1951, I drove my car to the British embassy with the intention of walking in and asking to see an intelligence officer . . . I wanted to tell my story. I needed one beckoning word or gesture to lead me on. Without it, I lacked the resolution to carry my impulse through.

But the least believable part of this book is the most important part of it: the account of his original recruitment as an active assistant of the Soviet Union. He claims that Blunt suddenly told him one day that 'our friends in the International' had assigned him a career as an American banker, 'to provide appraisals, economic appraisals, of Wall Street's plans to dominate the world economy'. Straight, his heroism already stirring, begs to be excused (Blunt 'praised me for not collapsing the night before'). In Moscow this news is received gravely, and he learns from Blunt that 'my appeal was nonetheless rejected'. Again he pleads to be released, and this time Stalin himself ponders the extraordinary quality of this twenty-year-old undergraduate, and decides he is too valuable to waste and that he must proceed to his station in America, the one concession being that he doesn't have to become a Wall Street banker (I hope he thanked Stalin nicely); for a time, he worked in the State Department instead.

From the beginning to the end of this rubbish, and indeed to the end of the book, there is not the slightest attempt on the part of Mr Straight to explain *why* he had to writhe and wrestle, appeal and appeal again (unsuccessfully), to be let off an appointment as a Soviet agent, and why he did not simply refuse and change the subject. It is just that 'The coil that held me was too distant to be visible, too dim to be identified, and, at the same time, too shameful to be revealed.' (I thought those last words might be a hint, but the author denies that he was a homosexual, so that can't be it. And what if he had been? Everybody else was, after all.)

No doubt the torrent of books about moles and spies, the Cambridge group and treason within MI6, will continue unabated. Certainly any hopes that this one might end it, by telling the whole story at last, are quickly dashed.

Elizabeth the First's 'great courtier' was not called Lord Cecil, there was no 'e' on Claud Cockburn's forename, if Mr Straight is going to call Emery Reeves 'an oily Messiah' he might at least spell his surname correctly, and there is no such place as Newcastle-under-Tyne, though I must say I wish there were.

Observer   March 13th, 1983

Will the real Vermeer
please stand up?

L AST WEEK A Manet was sold at Christie's in New York for $4 million. The same auction house, it is announced, is to sell in London some of the works of Mr Tom Keating, including pictures bearing his own signature as well as ones more imaginatively signed with names such as Titian and Rembrandt. (Reader, do not leap to conclusions; these may be perfectly genuine paintings by Nigel Titian and Kevin Rembrandt – artists less well known than their namesakes, perhaps, but not to be condemned out of hand for that.)

The first thing to be said is not the most important, but it might as well be said nevertheless: it is that I wouldn't half laugh if the Manet turned out to be by Mr Keating too. I shall not dwell upon the well-known disparity between what great artists of the past earned for their work and what dealers in those works now make out of them, because in the first place the argument is too worn, and in the second place it is largely spurious anyway, being usually employed for denunciations of the consumer society by artists who couldn't draw a triangle, never mind a real picture. Anyway, D. B. Wyndham Lewis said the last word from that point of view a long time ago:

Will the real Vermeer please stand up?

> Manet made so little monet,
> Dealers thought it rather fonet;
> As for Monet, some (not manet)
> Thought he wasn't making anet.

But this brings me back to a question that has haunted me for decades. Readers old enough to remember who van Meegeren was must bear with me while I remind the rest.

He was a Dutch art dealer and minor artist, who remained in the Netherlands throughout the Second World War and German Occupation, following his trade as best he could. After the war, he was prosecuted as a collaborator, the evidence being that he had sold to Goering a masterpiece by Vermeer, a huge 'Christ at Emmaus'. The picture was undoubtedly among Goering's loot, and it had certainly been sold to him or his agents by van Meegeren, so the case looked black. The dealer, however, pleaded not guilty, and his defence caused a considerable sensation. He claimed that instead of being condemned for collaborating with the enemy he should be commended for making fools of them, for, so far from the picture being by Vermeer, he had painted it himself.

His claim was greeted with considerable scepticism; the picture had been vouched for by leading art experts. Whereupon, van Meegeren caused an even greater sensation; he announced that if the court would order him to be provided in his prison with canvas, brushes, paint and a sufficiency of north light, he would be pleased to match the customer's sample by turning out another Vermeer on the same scale and with the same apparent authenticity. And that is precisely what he did. (When he did it, the Dutch authorities behaved shabbily; they prosecuted van Meegeren for forgery, and he was sentenced to a year in prison, where he died. Now I come to think of it, the British authorities behaved just as badly to the memorably named Mr Kempton Bunton, who stole the Goya 'Duke of Wellington' but later returned it unharmed. They prosecuted him for stealing the frame, which he had not returned, and he, too, was imprisoned. It is always dangerous, it seems, to make fools of the foolish.)

Now for van Meegeren's Question. As it happens, he did not ask it himself, though it enshrined what was obviously his view; it occurred in a play about the case, at one point in which van Meegeren is reflecting on the fact that his 'Christ at Emmaus' was universally accepted as genuine until he himself proved that it was a fake. I quote van Meegeren's Question from memory, but it went something like this:

> Yesterday, this picture was worth millions of guilders, and experts and art-lovers would come from all over the world and pay money to see it. Today, it is worth nothing, and nobody would cross the street to see it free. *But the picture has not changed.* What has?

I am blowed if I know, and the unblowed are warned that any attempt to provide the question with a snap answer will certainly come to grief. (Suppose, for instance, that van Meegeren had died before his trial; his Vermeer would presumably be accepted to this day. Moreover, he was able to get away with the original sale because there is evidence that Vermeer did paint such a picture, which had been presumed lost. So suppose that van Meegeren had died without revealing his secret, and the real Vermeer had then turned up; how would the experts have adjudicated between the two, and how would they have convinced anybody that they had made the right decision, whatever it was? Or suppose van Meegeren had left, to be opened after his death, a statement that his defence had been bogus, and that the disputed picture had been genuine after all? And suppose that that had happened, and the *genuine* genuine one had been found, and the experts had divided into two equal camps of supporters – which one would we have paid good money to see and be impressed by?)

The price of a picture is determined by supply and demand, within a framework of fashion, so there is no clue there; certainly some people will go to see a picture that has been sold for a record sum just *because* of the money it fetched, but they would also go to see, for the same reason, a giant uncut diamond or for that matter a very large pile of banknotes. The beauty of a picture ought not to be in the eye of the beholder, but that 'ought' is a fat lot of use in the face of van Meegeren's success, and for that matter a fat consolation for those who bought (and sold) Mr Keating's Palmers. If we stood in front of van Meegeren's Vermeer and felt profoundly affected by the majesty and power of the scene, just why would we stop feeling such things if a newsboy rushed into the gallery shouting that it had just been proved a fake?

Well, let me step into the witness-box myself. I have just published a book, in one chapter of which I go rattling on for pages about Vermeer's 'The Servant Pouring Milk' in the Rijksmuseum; I have gazed upon that picture countless times, for many hours in all, but I simply do not know what I would feel on my next visit if before it took place the picture was conclusively proved to be by Mr Denis Skinner, Lord Chief Justice Lane, or Mr Clive James.

If I would feel the same as I always have, then the identity of the artist is not important. In one sense, that is obviously true: there are some very great pictures which have never been attributed to any known artist. But suppose Mr Skinner, the LCJ or Mr James had been shown to have painted the picture, deliberately, in the style of Vermeer, which is what van Meegeren did: why would the authorship then start to matter – to matter so much, indeed, that I might no longer feel the same about it?

It is no use saying that there is a vast gulf between any masterpiece and any imitation of it, however meticulous. I have no doubt there is, but if we cannot see the difference – and successful art forgery would not exist if we could – what exactly does the difference consist of, apart from the fact that there must be one? Suppose that that four-million-dollar Manet did turn out to be a fake: the buyer could get his money back from Christie's, of course, but questions of legal liability plainly have nothing to do with artistic validity, so what would then be the standing of the oohs and ahs – quite genuine ones, I am sure – heard in the saleroom when it was held up before the bidding started?

Then again, what about a picture that has hung, neglected, in the corner of a gallery, for many years, attributed to a minor follower of Raphael? All of a sudden the greatest Raphael expert in the world takes a good look at it, and declares that it is from the master's own hand: all other experts look at it and agree, and the queues begin to form. Never mind the *motives* of the queuers: what has caused the difference in their *feelings* in front of the picture, which have changed overnight from casual interest to passionate devotion? (Remember van Meegeren: 'The picture has not changed. What has?')

The horrid truth seems to be that our response to art rests on a foundation much less secure than we like to think. I suppose it begins when we begin to learn about art, and all too often to learn about it in terms of hierarchies of eminence, so that Rembrandt=good is an equation fixed in our minds forever. But it is all too easy to believe, and millions do believe it, that his paintings are good because he is Rembrandt; in fact, his paintings are good because of the qualities to be found in them, and they would be no less good if they were by Smith,

Jones or Anon, yet the result of the equation-learning (the equivalent of the 'capes and bays' method of teaching geography when my mother was a girl) is that many visitors to an art gallery look first for the label which tells them who painted it, and then at the picture to see not what is there but what the label has told them.

If Rembrandt is good, then we are obliged to experience the appropriate response when looking at a picture he painted, and if we fail to experience it we are obliged to keep quiet. Conversely, when we are looking at a picture by not-Rembrandt, we accept that we are forbidden to feel the response appropriate to his work. Now: what happens when we are looking at a Rembrandt, with the right feelings, and we are told that it is a fake? The answer, surely, is the answer to van Meegeren's question: we switch off the feeling at once, and switch on the feeling appropriate to fakes – that is, an indignation made the more intense by the realisation that we have been fooled.

I have to say that I have never felt quite so tentative in offering an answer to a question in my life. But if that, or something like it, is not the answer to van Meegeren's riddle, what is? I think I had better leave it there, retreating in good order under the cover provided by Beachcomber's account of Captain Foulenough's brief career as the owner of a shady art gallery where hacks turned out rubbishy daubs which were then sold to credulous millionaires as examples of the finest modern art. One evening, Foulenough got drunk and signed a hideous abstract 'Tintoretto'. Even the sucker who was to be bamboozled into buying it jibbed at this, and the captain, thinking fast, insisted that the signature was in fact that of Tintorotto, an artist in the most *avant* of *gardes*. Thus reassured, the sucker paid up, and presumably van Meegeren, from that corner of Heaven reserved for those who have smitten the Philistines with the jawbone of an ass, chuckled quietly. My compliments to Tom Keating, and if he will only claim publicly to have painted the Manet there will be a bottle of champagne waiting for him *chez* Levin as soon as he cares to call.*

The Times   November 24th, 1983

*Mr Keating wrote to me, generously disclaiming any hand in the Manet. Shortly afterwards, alas, he died.

Educating Alfred

Bernard Shaw and Alfred Douglas: A Correspondence
edited by Mary Hyde*

IN 1965 MAX REINHARDT published the first of four projected volumes of the selected correspondence of Bernard Shaw; the second massive instalment followed in 1972, by which time it was already apparent that four volumes would not be enough. Then there was silence, broken only by rumours of a falling-out involving the editor, Professor Dan Laurence, whose work on the Letters had been a labour of scrupulous and sympathetic scholarship. Not long ago, there were rumours that Professor Laurence had had a falling-in, and that the long-silent engines were once again throbbing. I hope we may get Volume Three before too long; meanwhile, this rich, exotic feast should stave off the pangs of hunger.

I own to a powerful feeling, akin to the *furor Bloomsburiensis* that grips me whenever a new volume of Virginia Woolf's laundry-lists is published, that if the whole horrible *fin-de-siècle* circle of Alfred Douglas, R. H. Sherard, Robert Ross, Frank Harris and the rest had been boiled in their swaddling-clothes, the world would

*John Murray, 1982.

91

be a better place; I don't even think we would have lost very much if Wilde himself had been added to the pot.

Nor has this book caused me to change my mind; indeed, it strengthens my conviction that Douglas must have been one of the most dreadful men who ever lived. But he is safely dead and buried, and the warm, lucid sanity of Shaw combines in these pages with the febrile madness of Douglas to provide a meeting of two incompatible minds from which there emerges a fascinating and vivid portrait of a friendship (epistolary only, for they met only once, decades before the book begins) that illuminates not only the writers but the whole world of the Green Carnation.

Inevitably so, given that Douglas could only live in the past; though Wilde died in 1900, and the letters begin in 1931, Oscar dominates them from beginning to end. Again and again Douglas spends time justifying himself and condemning others; outbursts of rancour and spite alternate with sickening attempts at ingratiation. Throughout, Shaw remains calm, affable and generous; few men in all history other than the saints can have been so entirely free of grudges or resentment, though to Douglas he preached his admirable practice in vain:

Why has Heaven afflicted me with this infantile complex of yours which keeps you making 'a low-spirited noise,' like Mrs MacStinger's baby, down the ages because somebody has been unkind to you . . . I tell you, you must never have a grievance. Never excuse yourself, never deny, never explain, never moan; and seize every opportunity to . . . embrace every accusation and expose yourself to every reproach until your enemies are tempted to shift all the sympathy to your side by slapping your always-turned-other-cheek as hard as they can while you are

good-humouredly knocking them out with the disen-
gaged side.

The 'infantile complex' shot goes home; Douglas's side
of the correspondence removes any lingering doubt that
he was a child who never grew up, though I must say
that if I had been as beautiful as he was at eight (the book
is lavishly illustrated) I would have been tempted to
remain in Never-Never Land myself. All the same, he
was a poet of some quality, though not as good as he
thought he was or as Shaw tells him he is, and his
letters, though clearly not to be trusted as history (we
shall never finally know who did what, and with which,
and to whom), have a kind of seedy tragedy in them, so
desperate is he for respect or even affection:

> Your letter is epoch-making for me because you
> actually for the first time address me as 'dear Childe
> Alfred.' You have never done this before. You be-
> stowed the name on me but up till now you have
> never used it . . . I hope it won't be necessary for me
> to come to any more dark towers just now, as I've
> really been having a very bad time . . .

Shaw, of course, could not write a dull sentence if he
had wished to; Douglas has no gift of style, at any rate
in prose, though there is a kind of florid eagerness,
particularly when he is telling Shaw how humble,
devout and holy he is (he never stops praying for Shaw,
and constantly drops the names of St Jude and St
Antony of Padua as though they are his posh neighbours). But though Douglas often excites disgust, he
never provokes boredom, though I cannot say as much
for unseemly giggles, as, for instance, when he writes to
The Times (in May 1939) that in a war in which
England, France and Russia were allied against 'Christian nations like Italy, Germany and Spain' he 'would not

stand at England's side', on which the only possible comment is Oo-er.

Shaw's own cloven hoof is the Soviet Union, of course: 'I've been there. It is a paradise: no ladies and gentlemen . . . ' But there is little of such stuff here, and on so many subjects – Ireland, poetry, criticism, litiga-tion – he is wise, sound and witty all at once. Why he bothered with Douglas is a mystery: he cannot have been very interested in Wilde, and even if he was he could hardly have wanted to read the thousands of words in which Douglas went on and on and on insisting that Wilde, not he, had been responsible for the catastrophe, and that Wilde had betrayed him, not he Wilde. But Shaw's kindly tone never varies, even when Douglas asks him how one goes about getting a Civil List pension; he replies that Douglas must get a string of respectable testimonials to his penury and his literary achievements, though even Shaw cannot resist adding, 'As your literary achievements include a criminal libel on a cabinet minister and six months' expiation thereof, I have some doubt as to the success of this course.'

Observer　November 14th, 1982

Frankly impossible

The Playwright and the Pirate: Bernard Shaw and Frank Harris:
A Correspondence edited by Stanley Weintraub*

THE BOOM ROARS on; every day a new record is set
on the Shavian Stock Exchange. Not long ago we
had from the Bodley Head the first truly comprehensive
edition of his writings on music, 125,000 words longer
than the previously collected material. It was edited by
Professor Dan Laurence, who is once again at work on
the Collected Letters, and that mighty river is throwing
off tributaries as it flows; a few weeks ago I reviewed in
these pages Shaw's correspondence with Lord Alfred
Douglas, and here, hot on its heels, are the letters that
passed between him and Frank Harris. In addition, Mr
Michael Holroyd groans in biographical travail, and the
midwives declare he will eventually be delivered of a
prodigious number of volumes at a birth; meanwhile,
star-studded productions of *Man and Superman* and
Heartbreak House fill the Haymarket Theatre.

Has the pitcher gone once too often to the well? To
judge by the latest volume, certainly not. It is true that
Harris brought out less in Shaw than did Douglas,
probably because Harris was even more dreadful a man

*Colin Smythe, 1983.

than Bosie, and the sense of Shaw talking to a mirror is correspondingly stronger. But there is any amount of ripe fruit to be plucked here.

A few pages into this correspondence, the First World War has begun and Harris is in the United States, Britain having become a little too hot for him after a succession of financial and journalistic failures and lawsuits and a spell in jail; a few pages before the end, in 1931, Harris is dying in Nice, everywhere else in the world having become even hotter. Long before, Harris's star and Shaw's had crossed; Shaw's early reputation as a theatre critic had been made on the *Saturday Review*, of which Harris had been editor, but as Shaw rose to eminence as a playwright and sage, Harris sank to obscurity as a cadger, a blackmailer and a pornographer.

The final irony in the story is that Harris died, in desperate straits, just as he was finishing his biography of Shaw, which was intended to restore his fortunes. Shaw rewrote it for the benefit of Harris's penniless widow, and, as Professor Weintraub records, it sold 27,000 copies in London alone on the day of publication; Harris's curses on the world and its ingratitude must have been clearly audible from hell.

Harris had taken his character with him to America; more magazines waxed and waned, more shady transactions were entered upon. But he soon hit on a profitable idea; though his own books were hardly likely to be best-sellers, the inclusion of chunks of Shaw in them would make them saleable, so he began to cadge from Shaw words rather than money. Shaw saw through it at once, of course, but that extraordinary, grudgeless generosity did not fail; fourteen pages of this book consist of a 'letter' he wrote Harris about Wilde, knowing, and indeed intending, that Harris would shove it all into his own book on Oscar and blazon the Shaw contribution across the publishing heavens.

There is the same unpleasantly ingratiating tone in Harris's letters as there was in Douglas's, and Harris had even less of a sense of humour. Shaw was, as always, free with advice; the advice was genuine and practical; but it took no account of the self-destructive drive in the recipient. Douglas was determined to ensure that his name would be wiped out of the record, and achieved his aim by suing anybody who printed it; Harris was no less implacably bent on convincing such few influential men and women as did not already believe it that he was a thorough-paced blackguard, and got his wish finally with his two volumes of fantasy-biographical pornography, *My Life and Loves.*

Shaw called him nothing worse than 'pirate' and 'ruffian' (and Harris objected to both words), but that was Shaw's kindness again. Yet even Harris was not devoid of quality, just as Douglas was not wholly lacking in innocence:

I am writing this letter with one purpose and one purpose only. In my last book of Portraits I have told everyone what I think of Emma Goldman, one who has fought for the underdog for 30 odd years, and always with distinction. She was turned out of America, and turned again out of Russia, the Germans made life unpleasant for her, the French wouldn't have her except on sufferance, and at length we got her into England . . . I want you to call on her and make everything as nice for her as possible . . . You, too, can influence the Labour Government to make it easy for her in every way and I want you to do it. Take my word for it she is worth all the assistance you can give her and all the comfort too.

Shaw's own chief epistolary quality was his wit; there is a letter here, in which he parodies Harris's habit of boasting about the famous men to whom he gave a start in life, which is unfortunately too long to quote, but at which I laughed so loudly, while reading it in a hotel room at seven o'clock in the morning, that the man next door woke up and banged on the wall.

Towards the end, Harris's wretchedness, and his expression of it, recalls the benighted Corvo, and it is impossible to withhold pity from him, however much of his plight he had brought on himself; as for the recipient of his pleas, the more wretched Harris became, the better was Shaw's advice, and the greater his generosity. But the truth about Harris is more and worse than his flawed character; though he certainly had some flair as an editor, his own writing is dreadful – windy, lifeless and coarse.

Nobody could deserve the sordid fate of Frank Harris; but once he had decided he was a writer, and would earn his living at it, that fate was sealed. Douglas showed how much stir can be made with only a tiny talent, Harris how much mess can be made with virtually none at all. In both sets of correspondence, Shaw shows what can be achieved with genius and unremitting labour. On one point, then, both his correspondents were right: the world is unfair.

Observer   March 27th, 1983

A century of ecstasy and fear

I TELL YOU yet again, Banquo's buried; he cannot come out on's grave. Yet who would have thought the old man to have had so much blood in him? Or, to put it another way, Richard Wagner, who died a hundred years ago tomorrow, is still a living presence in a realm far wider than music, and is still capable of haunting our dreams, swallow we never so many sleeping-draughts before retiring.

Why should this be so? Why should one composer arouse feelings quite different from all other musicians who have ever lived, so that the nature of both the man and his music continues to be debated with a passion unknown elsewhere in the entire world of art?

This fact cannot be denied; I know very well, for instance, from repeated experience, that the letters I shall receive when these words appear will be of a character wholly different from those my readers are impelled to write when I offer my thoughts on Mozart or Schubert, Beethoven or Verdi. Wagner has been dead a hundred years, yet people still hate him, literally hate him and his music, as though he was a living presence haunting them, disturbing them, challenging them, worming his way into their thoughts and feelings.

The hate, I believe, is misplaced; but his effect is exactly what people irrationally believe it to be. He does

99

haunt us, he does disturb and challenge us, he does, above all, penetrate our psychological defences, throwing open doors and drawing back curtains that we strive to keep closed. In *The Flying Dutchman*, *Tannhäuser* and *Lohengrin* he announced, for those who had ears to hear, what he was going to do; in *Tristan*, *The Ring* and *Parsifal* he did it. What he did was to speak through his music of the greatest passions in the human psyche, feelings so dark and so powerful that we spend much of our waking and sleeping time devising means of chaining them safely. Hate, greed, theft, betrayal, murder, self-sacrifice, all-consuming love – these constitute his currency, and if we ask for change we get the voluptuousness in the first scene of *Tannhäuser*, the incest in *Die Walküre* and the retribution it brings, the curse in *Das Rheingold*, the rapture of Isolde, the terrible denial of Klingsor/Lucifer, the shadow-figures of Ortrud and Hagen, the redeeming epiphany of Parsifal, 'the holy fool, made wise through pity'.

Wagner depicts in music the act of physical love; he depicts no less vividly the blood of Christ. His symbols are as disturbing as his themes: a sword thrust to the hilt in a tree-trunk, gold stolen from its hiding-place beneath a river and fashioned into a talisman of infinite power, potions that induce forgetfulness of oath and honour, a god who breaks his word, a fire that need not burn, a wound that will not heal, a bird that warns, a staff that blooms, no fewer than four heroines and three heroes who can find the climax of relief only in death. Is it any wonder that, since we hate what we fear, so many people hate Wagner and his music?

But whether we hate his music or love it (and there are few who are indifferent to it), it will not let us alone. For a year now – and it will get worse, not better, as the months till summer pass – any gathering of music-lovers has sooner or later fallen to talking about the new *Ring* to be unveiled at Bayreuth in July, directed by

Peter Hall and conducted by Georg Solti; the river of
new books about him shows no sign of diminishing its
spate, let alone drying up (we are promised a *Who's Who*
of his work before the year's out, and sooner or later
someone will count every bar in *The Ring* and base a
series of cabbalistic calculations on the number); a
modern, sophisticated nation (with, it is worth pointing
out, probably a higher proportion of music-lovers
among its population than any other in the world)
continues to debate whether his music should be broad-
cast and played in concert halls, and attempts to perform
it are broken up by hooligans; and still he goes his way,
defying the limitations of time now he is dead as he
defied the limitations of the world (not to mention his
character) while he was alive, and causing generations of
visitors to Wahnfried to listen in terror for the sound of
knocking coming from his tomb. Mark my words, one
of these days – tomorrow, perhaps – it will be heard.

And yet for anyone who can bear it, or who needs it,
his music, though it cannot carry us as high as Mozart,
Schubert or Beethoven do, can take us deeper into a
flood of musical ecstasy than even they. When the
pilgrims return at the end of *Tannhäuser* with their
astounding news, when the shepherd's pipe at last
breaks into rejoicing on Tristan's island, when the gods
go a-begging into their doomed magnificence as the
curtain falls on *Rheingold*, when the spear that pierced
Christ's side heals the unending agony of Amfortas,
when Daland's crew break into their shanty, when
Siegmund and Sieglinde hymn the spring and their love,
when my hair stands on end as the music curdles from
rejoicing into murder in the very last bars of Act II of
Götterdämmerung, when Siegfried's kiss awakens Brünn-
hilde to greet the sun – why, when any of these things
happen to me in an opera-house, I know that there is yet
another reason for the uniqueness of Richard Wagner:
that for all the doubt and fear and pain he awakens in his

101

listeners, he is one of the greatest and most original artists the world has ever known, and his music will live as long as there are mouths and hands to sing and play it, and ears to hear it.

The more knowledgeable among you will by now have noticed that I have so far mentioned only nine of the ten operas of Wagner's maturity; the more perceptive will guess that I have been saving the tenth for a special purpose. So I have; for *The Mastersingers* is the spear of salvation for the Amfortas-wound of Richard Wagner, and if all his other works were swept into eternal oblivion, leaving only that one, we would have no right to complain. *The Mastersingers* is sunlit throughout; there is a villain, but he is filled only with sawdust, there are star-crossed lovers, but the stars shine for them in the end, there are broken heads in the night, but they will heal by morning, there is a philosopher as wise and benevolent as Sarastro, who, like Sarastro, resolves the discords of the world and establishes the harmony of the universe.

There is nothing to be afraid of in *The Mastersingers*, nothing to hate; nothing is here for tears, nothing to weep or knock the breast. There is only a great affirmation of man's place in the world, a place bounded by work, love and song, and whenever I see it, even in an indifferent performance, I leave the opera-house with my heart full of the peace that passeth all understanding.

I most fervently wish Richard Wagner to remain in his grave tomorrow. But if he must rise again, with twenty mortal murders on his crown, and push us from our stools, let him come armed with the serenity and splendour of *Die Meistersinger von Nürnberg*, and all shall be forgiven him for at least another hundred years.

The Times   February 12th 1983

Thoughts on a cold pavement

IT WAS FIVE minutes past curtain-time, and I was beginning to wonder (knowing that at this particular theatre they tend to be punctual in starting) whether all was not well with the leading lady, when a familiar figure appeared in front of the curtain and said, with a kind of authoritative charm, 'Ladies and gentlemen, I'm afraid we have a rather special kind of problem this evening, and we must ask you to leave the building at once – the police will notify you when you may return.'

We rose, and proceeded in an orderly fashion to the exits. (Two members of the audience were seen *running*, but it was agreed by the rest of us that they must have been foreigners.) In the hour or so we spent on the pavement in weather that would have frozen a penguin, it was possible to reflect on certain questions of the day in a particularly concentrated manner.

First, it was noticeable that nobody at all was in doubt as to the meaning of the management's words, though 'bomb', 'telephone-call' and 'danger' were not among them. Second, nobody grumbled, except at the perishing cold; those who might be presumed to have caused us our discomfort were not abused *in absentia*, nor was there any sense of outrage. Nobody even denounced the management for shutting the cloak-rooms as soon as the evacuation order was decided upon, and nobody ventured the opinion that they should have treated the telephone-call as the hoax it was overwhelmingly likely (and in the event proved) to be.

Next, it was apparent once more that an emergency always brings out the friendliness in the British; people who had never met before were talking to each other within a few minutes, and I daresay that in years to come there will be devoted couples telling their friends 'We met in a bomb-scare.' (Kenneth Tynan, reviewing *The Iceman Cometh*, said that in the fourth hour the atmosphere in the theatre was exactly like that in a wartime air-raid shelter, with 'complete strangers offering one another wine-gums'.)

And finally, I had the melancholy and useless satisfaction of knowing that I solved this problem some years ago, and publicly announced my solution, too, though I did not expect anything to be done (nor was it), because the people who would have had to do the doing were those in charge of the telephone-service; I have no expectation that British Telecom will be any more heedful than their predecessors, but I may as well repeat my solution anyway. It is to change from our present telephone system of what is technically known as 'Calling party release' to 'Called party release'. At present if I call you and you hang up but I don't, you remain connected to me; if the system were inverted, the bomb-hoaxer (or genuine bomb planter for that matter) would hang up, having given his ominous message, only to find that he was still connected to his victim, thus enabling him to be traced promptly and with certainty.

Meanwhile, a few conclusions can be drawn. It is little more than a decade since serious urban terrorism in civilised Western societies began; before that, there was nothing to worry about, apart from the internecine wars of Chicago gangsters, a brief flurry by the IRA just before the Second World War, and the random actions of those who were collectively known as anarchists and who were so little regarded as a threat to society that the type was always portrayed as a comic figure with a cloak, a fringe beard, and a round 'infernal machine' which was gently smoking and invariably labelled 'Bomb'.

Nous avons changé tout cela. And yet . . . Air piracy is of the same modernity as bomb-planting, but we no more grumble at, or find in any way surprising, the searches of luggage and person at airports than we get hysterical, or even seriously cross, when we are turned out of a theatre. Every now and again a real bomb goes off in a city far removed from areas of endemic political violence; unless it causes large numbers of casualties (particularly among horses) it now makes hardly a ripple across the public consciousness. Baader-Meinhof Gangs, Red Army Fractions, Weathermen – they have killed people from time to time, but not more, I imagine, than are struck by lightning, or indeed are accounted for by the Charles Mansons and Dennis Nilsens and their like. (There are as many 'ordinary' murders in Los Angeles in a single year as there have been corpses in Northern Ireland attributable to terrorism since the present 'Troubles' began.)

Of course, the hoaxers have battened on the activities of the killers in a manner which is unique to our time, and there must be dozens of false alarms to every real emergency. That makes life more troublesome, as those who went wheezing about their business the day after our pavement vigil in the cold could testify; if it comes to that, there were, no doubt, people who had to leave before the end of the performance to catch their last trains and buses, though if the curtain had gone up on time they could have stayed to the end.

What does all that amount to? A few horrible deaths and injuries; a far greater quantity of inconvenience patiently and light-heartedly borne (when the 'sniffer' dogs arrived – gentle-looking Labradors – and lolloped into the theatre as into a Disney cartoon, they were greeted by laughter rather than cheers); and, surely, the defeat, almost total, of the enemy.

Are lives seriously disrupted or made less worth living by such trivia? In Lebanon, life must be hardly bearable; in Belfast it must be at least very different; but I am not talking of the centres of violence, only of the violence in those countries where it is either random (as in West Germany and Italy) or designed (as in mainland Britain) to bring pressure to bear on those who will ultimately have to decide whether the centres of violence can be pacified by political action.

The truth that emerges is very encouraging. First in the United States, then in Western Germany, then increasingly in Italy, the political urban terrorists have been reduced to tiny handfuls of disheartened wretches. They have been reduced by patient, unwavering work on the part of democratic authorities and their forces of order, and by the refusal of the general public either to panic or to demand that peace should be achieved by surrender.

There was neither fear nor anger on that chilly pavement the other night; only an instinctive understanding that the price we were paying to keep our society not only free but calm and ordered was ludicrously small compared to what it was buying. If the hoaxer who turned us out into the night is caught, I think six months or so in the hoosegow would be appropriate, besides tending to discourage others like him, for it is not actually *fun* to freeze to death even if everybody around you is freezing to death as well. But if we have to waste a few minutes at an airport, or get cold outside a theatre once a year, or even be startled from time to time by a loud bang followed by the sound of fire-engines and ambulances, civilised life will not become impossible, or even be seriously diminished.

And even if we have to put up with those things for decades to come, that will remain true. Why, when in the interval of the resumed performance I met the spokesman who had made the original ominous announcement, I shook his hand warmly, in token that all was forgiven. And in truth there was nothing to forgive.

The Times December 9th, 1983

Love's state secrets

II. H. Asquith: Letters to Venetia Stanley
edited by Michael and Eleanor Brock*

O NE SUNDAY MORNING in the early spring of 1912,
Herbert Asquith, who was then sixty years old and
had been Prime Minister for four years (he was to hold
the office for four more), fell totally in love, in a single
instant, with Venetia Stanley, one of his daughter
Violet's friends and contemporaries, thirty-five years
his junior. Or so it is said, not least by him, and since in
the course of the following thirty-four months he wrote
her at least 560 letters, almost every single one of which
pours out love and adoration in terms unqualified by
any apparent recollection that he was a married man as
well as Prime Minister, my claim that I don't believe a
word of it may seem – indeed, may *be* – difficult to
sustain.

The evidence is certainly formidable. In the first four
months of 1915 alone he wrote 186 letters to Venetia;
sometimes there were three in a day, and on occasion
four. He wrote them from his country house, from 10
Downing Street, from trains and motor-cars, from the
houses of his friends, from the Front Bench of the

*Oxford, 1982.

108

House of Commons, from the Cabinet Room *while the Cabinet was in session*, under the noses of his hostesses, his colleagues, his opponents and his wife.

His recklessness in the affair (it was apparently never consummated, and from the tone of his letters it seems very unlikely that the thought of a physical relationship ever crossed his mind) suggests that he was not simply drunk on love (or liquor – he did have a drink problem) but deranged; from the outbreak of the Great War he was sending her the most secret military information, much of which, in enemy hands, could have led directly to the rout and slaughter of British troops, and most of these letters went by ordinary post.

When the letters begin Asquith was in the throes of the struggle over Home Rule; he and his Government, unable to square the circle, faced the certainty of civil war in Ireland (Redmond takes on a greater stature through the evidence of these extraordinarily candid documents, and Carson becomes even more repugnant), from which he and the Liberals were saved only by the outbreak of war in Europe – one of the greatest ironies of all the irony-strewn history of Anglo-Irish relations.

Even as early as Letter 31 his indiscretion was astounding: he was, for instance, eager to send her in advance the crucial paragraph about Home Rule from the King's Speech in February 1914, and only refrained because she expressed no interest in it. 'There is nothing (as you know)', he wrote, 'that I would not show you: so great and deep is my trust.' (There is no evidence that she ever betrayed it.)

In effect, these letters constitute Asquith's detailed, intimate political diary, day by day and sometimes hour by hour. They thus constitute a source-book of British history for the period covered that will be of enormous and enduring value, and the story they tell, public and private, is of the most enthralling nature; readers in a hurry are warned that for all its 600 pages the book is impossible to skip.

There are wonderfully vivid portraits of the politicians and others around him: Churchill, impetuous, dashing, obstinate; the creepy Simon (Asquith calls him 'Sinless John' or 'the Impeccable'); Lloyd George, up to his neck in conspiracies; Arnold Bennett, 'a bounder of the first degree'; Kitchener, who was plainly half mad, and Jacky Fisher, who was at least three-quarters so (he wanted to shoot all the German prisoners-of-war in Britain); and the Jewish Edwin Montagu, 'the Assyrian' to Asquith, who courted Venetia before the period of the correspondence, resumed his suit towards its end (at least once they were both writing to her during the same Cabinet meeting, and Montagu even complains that Winston won't shut up long enough for him to finish the letter) and emerged victorious, breaking Asquith's heart in the process. (He thought Montagu unworthy of Venetia, not least, apparently, because he was a Jew.)

Even at the height of the Irish crisis, the Austrian ultimatum to Serbia that led to the war, the chaos in the early days of the BEF and the retreat from Mons, the Dardanelles tragedy itself, Asquith, recording history and his feelings together, wrote steadily on, as indeed he played relentlessly on at bridge and even golf; the flavour of a vanished world in which there was always enough time is beautifully conveyed. So is the strength he found in Venetia:

> It has been given I suppose to few men to go through such a succession of 'crises' in the same space of time; you have been a stay and refreshment to me in them all; and during this last 12 months with its almost miraculous series of emergencies I have come more & more to rely and rest upon you, and you have never failed me either in counsel or in love.

110

How much he depended on her is made clear from the profound depressions into which he fell if the post was late or, even worse, if there was no letter from her in it.

But love? Certainly he believed that that was what he felt:

> My love for you has grown day by day & month by month & (now) year by year: till it absorbs and inspires all my life. I could not if I would, and would not if I could, arrest its flow, or limit its extent, or lower by a single degree its intensity, or make it a less sovereign and dominating factor in my thoughts and purposes and hopes . . . It enables me in the daily stress of almost intolerable burdens & anxieties to see visions & dream dreams . . .

Now those are surely the words of a man in love not with a woman but with an idealised *feeling* of love; as the tide of words mounts higher it becomes plain that the whole thing is a beautiful construction, built on a real foundation (of his need for a confidante) but having no more substance than any cloud-capped tower or insubstantial pageant that leaves not a wrack behind.

Asquith, as he says himself, saw visions and dreamed dreams; though I am unable to believe in them, they give a strange and hauntingly ethereal quality to a fascinating and massively detailed account of the last days of Liberal England, and of the man who presided over the end of a world. Venetia stares out from the jacket, a cool beauty with marvellous eyes; any reader of this tremendous book will feel forever indebted to her for inspiring it.

Observer November 28th, 1982

They ache and we suffer

IF ANTON WEBERN were alive today (which thank the Lord he's not, sir) he would be a hundred; set off by the centenary, his music has been raging through Europe like influenza, and many of the victims have developed hideous secondary symptoms in the form of Berg, Stockhausen and even Varese. Prognosis in most cases is grave, and where Boulez and Schoenberg have set in, little hope can remain; at the Barbican on Tuesday, for instance, the Vienna Philharmonic under Mehta were unable to fill the hall, despite the fact that the second half of the concert consisted of the Schubert C major Symphony (a marvellously sonorous and exciting performance, incidentally), because the first half was devoted entirely to Webern. (The one thing that can be said in favour of Webern is that his works are mercifully short; each of the *Five Orchestral Pieces*, for instance, consists of not much more than three plinks and a plonk, and even the *Six Orchestral Pieces*, which figured in Tuesday's programme and are massive structures by comparison, were all over in less than ten minutes the lot, with an average for each item of five plinks, two plonks and a grrrrrr.)

We can, I think, safely take it that no man in his senses wants to listen to this stuff or enjoys it when he does so; some think they *ought* to listen to it, but even the writer of Tuesday's programme notes ('. . . shook off the last trappings of tonality . . . skeletal thematicism . . . revolutionary compression . . . steadily accelerating to a catastrophic disintegration . . . ') made it sound as though the First Principle of Medicine – the nastier it tastes the more good it is doing you – was being applied. So what was it doing up front in the concert, making us wait three-quarters of an hour for Schubert?

Mark, I do not suggest that Webern was a charlatan, let alone that Schoenberg and Berg were; indeed, I do not think that even Stockhausen is having us on. They make these horrible noises because they feel like it, not to impress Mr Hans Keller, and it is no more an answer to say that the hall would have been *entirely* empty without the Schubert in the bill than it is an equal and opposite answer to say that Berio must be a genius because at the first performance of Beethoven's Third Symphony somebody in the audience shouted, 'I'd give another *kreutzer* if the thing would stop.' This subject is a minefield sown with undistributed middles, and great care must be taken while travelling through it.

All the same, these people *do* make horrible noises, and nobody enjoys listening to them. What has happened?

First, steadily growing throughout our era, is the belief that art is not something to be enjoyed, but something through which we are to suffer. But that is not true. Certainly tastes differ, and the fact that I would not give fourpence a square yard for the entire works of Francis Bacon does not affect his prices; all the same, I have never seen, in any gallery showing his pictures, any expression on the faces of those looking at them other than revulsion and rejection, and neither have you.

The defenders of the Sacher-Masoch Theory of Art will say that we live in an ugly world, full of moral and political dissonance and distortion, and that it is the artist's duty to reflect that world; whence not only the nasty noises, the hideous paintings and the New Nihilism of the 'committed' playwrights, but also such lunacy as action painting and aleatoric music. What these people forget is that the world has always been ugly, cruel and capricious, yet only in very recent times has art begun to insist that those qualities are the most significant and that art must take on their nature.

Why is random art – paint flung from buckets, music garnered from radio atmospherics, novels published loose-leaved, to be shuffled before reading – such nonsense? Do you suppose that Shakespeare didn't know that the world could fly apart at any moment, and that the Wars of the Roses had ended only eighty years before he was born? Do you imagine that Rembrandt, because he lived in Holland, had never heard of the Massacre of St Bartholomew, only thirty-four years before he was born? Do you think that Bach would have enjoyed himself if Charles XII had come to tea? Do you believe that Dostoievsky thought life was a bowl of cherries? Of course such artists knew that they had to assimilate suffering and refine it into their art, that they had to face ugliness before they could conceive beauty, that the ice of the world is eternally thin, and will always creak and groan and roar in travail as the artist tiptoes his way across it.

But that is why art is centripetal, and the artist's duty to keep it so. Art is the integument that binds humankind, truth and beauty together, and it is able to serve that purpose because, and only because, it can keep simultaneously in view the lesser truth that the world can fall to pieces at any moment and the greater truth that it will not.

The ugliness, and – much more significant – the triviality, of so much of modern art is a reflection of the fact that so many artists have ceased to be capable of that dual vision, and that some deny that the duality exists at all, or even maintain that the only truth about the universe is that it is charged and primed with disintegration. (What was it that led to the present danger of nuclear annihilation if not the splitting of the atom, that ultimate, hideous, unforgivable impiety of putting asunder that which God had joined together?)

This is the mistake of the false prophets, who strive ceaselessly (but, happily, in vain) to lead the common people astray. I am myself one of the common people, and it is on their behalf and at their unanimous request that I am speaking today, just as on Tuesday night I acted as their representative when, while listening to the Webern, I made a face as of one who has just swallowed a quince, and waited patiently until Schubert arrived with his great hymn to wholeness – a wholeness so complete that it can even encompass fragmentation, just as the Fifth Symphony of Beethoven is a hymn to the light so overwhelming that it even contains darkness.

Atonality was the great barrier reef on which modern music shattered, as the stream-of-consciousness was the torpedo that sank the novel and abstraction the anaesthetic that put painting to sleep. But these things are not just techniques; they are a direct consequence of the sickness in the artist's soul, a sickness which denies the duty which he previously shouldered uncomplainingly from Giotto to Picasso, from Monteverdi to Britten, from Rabelais (or Homer if you like) to Thomas Mann, from Aeschylus to Chekhov. All life, and therefore all art, strives towards harmony. Why does a playwright like Stoppard, a novelist like Naipaul, a painter like Matta, stand out so tremendously today? Because artists like these do know the artist's duty: to face the void without flinching, to declare that the world will yet be saved, and to weave their single strand of the great rope – made of form and meaning equally – that holds the universe together. And I know this: another century hence, no one will think of celebrating Webern's bicentenary, because he will be utterly forgotten. But the C major Symphony of Schubert will still be as fresh, as glorious, and as true as ever.

The Times   December 17th, 1983

Exit to the unthinkable

THE ARGUMENTS, LEGAL and ethical, over the Voluntary Euthanasia Society and its activities will not end with the court case recently concluded. Miss Gillian Tindall, a few days later, put the case, on this page, for the Voluntary Euthanasia Society and its wish to disseminate information that will help intending suicides to achieve their aim. Now I propose to put the case against it.

I must first draw attention to the title of the society's do-it-yourself suicide manual; it is called *A Guide to Self-Deliverance*. This rich and striking example of Newspeak suggests that the society's leaders are by no means so sure of themselves as they would like to think, let alone as they would like *us* to think. The booklet, after all, as is admitted by the society (it is not available to non-members, or even to members under twenty-five), gives advice to those who wish to commit suicide; it would surely be better, therefore, to call it *A Guide to Suicide* or, even more plainly and honestly, *How to Kill Yourself*. This question of nomenclature is not the most important, but it is not at all unimportant, and should be borne in mind; 'Self-Deliverance' in this context is a sanitised word, a perfumed word, an advertiser's or vendor's word, and we have the right to ask why it was used.

117

Miss Tindall, in her article, quoted a remark made by one of the counsel in the legal proceedings, presumably counsel for the defendants; he spoke of 'the sovereign, unalienable and absolute right to die'. That, clearly, is the heart of the argument, and I shall return to it, but first there are some other matters to get out of the way.

Suicide is no longer a crime; it used to be the one offence on the Statute Book that was punishable only if it was unsuccessful, which was widely portrayed as absurd, but obviously the point of the criminal law was to put a barrier before those who would help others to kill themselves (the survivor of a suicide pact was sometimes prosecuted), which was anything but absurd in view of the danger that, for instance, elderly and inconvenient relatives might be steered, not altogether with their approval, in a direction from which they would not return.

At this point it must be said that the Voluntary Euthanasia Society certainly does not need me to draw to its attention the dangers of which I have given one example; it is fully cognisant of them, and has proposed practical ways to minimise them. What it cannot do, however, is to predict the consequences of legalising, not suicide (which is already legal), but any form, however controlled and safeguarded, of helping to their deaths individuals who wish to die but are unable, say by reason of physical disability, to commit suicide unaided. (This was, of course, the central theme of Mr Brian Clark's successful play *Whose Life Is It Anyway?*)

But if there are rigid and inescapable safeguards in any such proposals, what untoward consequences can there be? In the answer to that lies one of the most terrible truths about mankind. Once we legalise assisted suicide we have altered, significantly and irrevocably, the standpoint from which we observe such matters, and once we have done that, things which were previously quite unthinkable move into an area in which it is possible to think them. And having been thought, sooner or later they, too, will be proposed. No reader of these words needs me to say precisely what I am talking about, but the Fallacy of the Altered Standpoint is the sign-manual of our bloodstained century, and I do not believe that the smallest countenance should be given to suggestions, no matter how scrupulous, sensible and reputable their advocacy, which would give any further credence to that fallacy.

All this, however, concerns the social and legal aspects of suicide, and these, though important, do not constitute the essence of the real question, which is: was Hamlet right when he said that the Almighty had fixed his canon 'gainst self-slaughter?

It should be noted first that almost all of the great religions set their face against suicide; for Roman Catholics it is a sin even to contemplate it (Dante puts the suicides in the seventh circle of Hell). Nor is it difficult to see why this should be so; all religions teach, in one way or another, that our lives are not ours but God's, and may not, therefore, be thrown away. But does it make sense to argue that suicide is wrong for those who have no religious beliefs to restrain them?

Here we must tread carefully. I suppose most people have known suicides; a surprisingly large number have contemplated taking their own lives. Who are we to judge, say, those who are suffering from some incurable and agonising disease, or who face some other insupportable misery or loss, and anticipate the inevitable by their own hand? Well, of course I do not judge them, in the sense of condemning or censuring them; but is it impossible to say that they may be mistaken in their belief that they have that 'sovereign, unalienable and absolute right'?

To begin with there is the extraordinary and surely meaningful fact that *nothing* is hopeless. There is no 'incurable' disease known to medicine that is without its

119

cases of spontaneous remission, no bereavement so cruel that it can never be accepted and survived, no disgrace so total that it cannot be lived through. In every category of suicide there have been those who, with the same overwhelming justification, have stayed their hands, and not regretted it. (We have no means of knowing how many of those who have not stayed their hands have regretted it too late.) Second, there is the no less extraordinary and meaningful fact that the life instinct is the most powerful and tenacious in human kind. Consider the unending and hopeless privations, tortures, degradations, that men and women have survived, solely because of the limitless strength of the determination to stay alive – a determination which sometimes works far below a consciousness that cries out to die. Look at that most haunting image of our time, the crowd of living skeletons in the liberated concentration camps who, by all imaginable tests, should have long previously given up the fight to live, yet who insisted on staying alive for a dawn they had no reason to believe would ever come. Look at the injuries that the human body has sustained and survived, the poverty and hunger, the rejection and hatred; why, even John Merrick, the 'elephant man', who could not possibly have foreseen the unique accident that saved him, did not take his own life, despite a condition among the most terrible it has ever been given to a human being to endure.

'Given'; have I begged the question, or instinctively answered it? I am one of those – and we are many today – who, without any definable set of religious beliefs, yet cannot persuade themselves that life is an accident, the universe random, and both without ultimate meaning. If life has meaning, derived from a universe that itself makes sense, then we surely have a duty to use all the life that we have, to accept, and to learn from, whatever may befall us, to ignore or reject nothing, to believe that understanding and enlightenment may come to us between the stirrup and the ground, or indeed in the very moment of death. But until that moment, I believe that we must carry the vessel of life over even the stoniest ground without deliberately spilling it, and history is full of men and women who have obeyed that command whatever the cost. Am I not right in believing that there is only one suicide in the New Testament? If I am, I hardly think I need tell you his name.

The Times May 5th, 1983

Free speech is expensive

THERE MUST COME a time in every red-blooded boy or girl's life when the desire to throw eggs at Mr Michael Heseltine becomes overpowering; even I, conscious as I am of the dignity demanded by my years and eminence, would feel strange impulses stirring if I were to bump into him outside a dairy. Hurling paint at him would not be my style, though I agree that it is not easy to draw any kind of moral distinction between the two types of missile, and I can see how the less indelible assault could lead to the more. But today's question is not whether it would be *pleasant* to turn Mr Heseltine into a vividly-coloured omelette, but whether it is *right* to do so, and while doing so to prevent him, by yelling and screaming and stamping, from offering his opinions to those who have invited him to address them.

On the whole, and by and large, and taking one consideration with another, I think it is not. As it happens, Mr Heseltine must be better able to endure the eggs and paint than most; he has lots and lots and *lots* of suits in his wardrobe, and can easily afford the most expensive and deep-cleansing shampoo on the market. As it further happens, I have no doubt at all that the momentary discomfort of the pelting was very heavily outweighed by his delight in the knowledge that nothing could have been better calculated to produce sympathy and assent for his views than the attempt to suppress them by violence. Indeed, if the slippery monsignor had any sense, he would start to hint that Mr Heseltine had hired the demonstrators himself.

But the fact that Mr Heseltine and his views on the necessity of nuclear defence have gained by the actions of those who sought to cause him loss is not the most important here. Nor, even, is the fact that, as the picture of him surrounded by a phalanx of policemen showed, he was lucky that nothing worse than paint and eggs happened to him. What *is* most important is that people who disagreed with his opinion sought, not to express that disagreement, but to silence that opinion. By all accounts, they largely succeeded, but it would make no difference if they had not; the attempt and not the deed confounds us.

There is no comfort to be found in the obvious truth: that those who demand exclusive rights of expression for their own views, and seek to deny that right to the expression of contrary views, realise, however deeply they bury the realisation, that their views are mistaken. The reason that there is no comfort in the truism is that it makes no difference to what actually happens when those of totalitarian tendencies have the power to impose their tendencies on those with democratic ones. In totalitarian states no other views are allowed; that indeed is how 'total' gave birth to 'totalitarian'. But a mob determined and able to silence a cabinet minister is a totalitarian state in miniature, and its weapons – noise, missiles and ultimately bodily violence – though they are obviously lesser in degree than the weapons of concentration camp and torture chamber, are the same in kind: they are the means by which the enemies of freedom destroy freedom in whatever area they control.

Of course, there are those who think Mr Heseltine is too smooth for his, or our, own good; they must inevitably find it difficult to work up much enthusiasm for his right to free speech. Even I would have been happier in my work today if it had been St Francis of Assisi or the Princess of Wales who had been painted, egged and howled down. But as I have so often pointed out, the only people who really need their right to free speech defended are those who dismay us by exercising it, and since it is Mr Heseltine, and not Mother Teresa of Calcutta or Sir Woodrow Wyatt, who suffered the suppression of that right, it is he who today must have it defended, even if some of the defenders will do so with the words of Edmund in *King Lear*: 'Now, gods, stand up for bastards.'

Let us not dismiss the episode – which, incidentally, was not the first of its kind recently, and will not be the last – by saying that students must be allowed to let off steam, that golden boys and girls all must, like chimney-sweepers, grow up eventually, that a gang of nasty youths with boils and puppy-fatted girls with lank hair are not going to destroy civilisation as we know it. Students have made more noise than the neighbourhood can readily accommodate since Erasmus of Rotterdam had his first hangover, but I think that it is only in the last half-century or so that they have acquired the kind of intolerance which faced Mr Heseltine, and only in the last twenty years that they have put that intolerance into practice in the knowledge that no serious rebuke, let alone punishment, will follow.

Nor let us put up with the inevitable cant about feelings running so high among these idealistic lads and lasses as they contemplate the horrors of nuclear weapons that they – no doubt mistakenly, perhaps even wrongly, but above all understandably – allowed their admirable passion to issue in actions which could just possibly be thought, at least by the very severest of critics, to constitute a slight infringement of free speech. Apart from the fact that it *is* cant, it had nothing to do with what happened, which was that some people who had decided that Mr Heseltine should not be allowed to speak went along to his meeting with the prior intention of making sure that he did not, and took eggs and paint with the prior intention of throwing them at him.

Now: what are we going to do about this? The suppression of free speech is certainly not confined to the universities; there is a good deal of it about in the real world too, with such totalitarian organisations as the National Front and its mirror image the Socialist Workers Party, determined that those who disagree with them shall not be heard. It is difficult for the law to enforce the right of free speech (though university authorities are adequately equipped with powers to discipline those who physically obstruct that right, and might occasionally try exercising those powers); to assault a speaker is certainly a criminal offence, but to drown his words with shouting is only very dubiously so (as in the offence of 'the use of words whereby a breach of the peace might be occasioned'), and in any case the law should only be used in these matters as a final recourse when all others have failed.

Somehow, we have got to get, or to get back, to a situation in which anything that may *lawfully* be said in public may *actually* be said in public. A heavy share of the responsibility for the fact that that is not at present true lies with those Labour politicians and trade union leaders who have encouraged or condoned or associated themselves with defiance of the law, at Clay Cross, or Grunwick, or – as is happening now – the refusal to abide by a court order on unlawful picketing. But in the end the only way to assert the right of free speech is to assert the free speech itself. If speakers have to be escorted into and out of their meetings by the police, escorted they must be. If they take several hours to finish a speech because only for five seconds in every five minutes can they be heard, then everybody on the platform and off it will have to be patient. If loudhailers are needed for them to be heard, let there be loudhailers. If stewards, *using no more than reasonable and necessary force*, have to eject those who come not to listen but to prevent others listening, then out the preventers must go. If the totalitarians abandon words and resort to missiles, then any who are observed to be using the missiles must be prosecuted. If there are those among us who claim to choose which laws they shall obey, and which they shall break, the law must disillusion them.

That is not an exciting programme, and it will not be quickly completed. But however dull its course, and however long it takes, it had better be embarked upon soon. Mr Heseltine may not count the cost of his dry-cleaning bills. But the cost of what we lose if he has to pay many more of them will be higher than any of us can afford.

The Times   November 22nd, 1983

Speaking in tongues

Daphne into Laurel: Translations of Classical Poetry from Chaucer to the Present edited by Richard Stoneman*

IT IS POSSIBLE to learn a great deal about one country from the way it translates the literature of another, and indeed from its choice of what foreign literature to translate. Almost all French Shakespeare, for instance, is bad, including the Gide *Hamlet*, and it is bad because the French literary tradition is so un-Shakespearian that the translators have generally been quite unable to take his measure. Similarly, the strangeness of Goethe is precisely the kind of strangeness that bemuses the anglophone mind; I have never yet come across a really satisfactory *Faust* in English, and I do not expect to.

Latin and Greek literature provides the perfect test, first because all Western literature is steeped in it, and second because every age has translated it afresh, so that we can watch, through this serviceable prism, a nation's mind unfolding over the centuries. Mr Stoneman's anthology is comprehensive and informatively and carefully edited (apart from a shocking misquotation of Wordsworth); he tips his hat to Chaucer and ends with C. H. Sisson and Ted Hughes, but the bulk of his

*Duckworth, 1982.

127

collection comes, as one would expect, from the six-teenth, seventeenth and eighteenth centuries. He has mercifully omitted most of the merely worthy (Beer-bohm drew a cartoon of a 'Statesman of the Olden Time, making without wish for emolument a flat but faithful version of the Georgics in English hexameters') but rightly includes a few examples of the downright dreadful, such as the Homer of Arthur Hall, published about 1590, which includes the memorable line 'Nine days throughout right brave they feast, the banquets were not bad.'

Most of the greatest English poets before modern times essayed classical translation (itself a comment on the changing place of the classics in this country's education), and at times practically every poet in the land: Mr Stoneman says of the seventeenth century that 'by the Restoration, translation was nothing short of a craze'.

Latin, on the whole, preceded Greek; English Hellen-ism is a fairly late flower. Chapman's Homer appeared when the argument over metre was at its height, and men went to battle for the hexameter as fiercely as Don Quixote for Dulcinea. His use of the dangerously cumbersome fourteener for the *Iliad* (published first) proved an *ignis fatuus* for some who followed, and he abandoned it himself in the *Odyssey*, for the pentameter, which on the whole has carried the day.

We all know what Keats felt on first looking into Chapman's Homer; but what did he find there? He found not only a great poet engaging his mind with that of another, but a man of his time who used Homer as a mirror, and saw his own and his time's face in it. It is obvious in the case of some translators that their achievements could stand independent of the original; a reader who had never heard of Homer would not deduce his existence from Chapman, and still less from Pope. The editor is severe on Bentley's 'A very pretty

128

poem, Mr Pope, but you must not call it Homer,' but the fact remains that it must *not* be called Homer, because Homer was not an eighteenth-century Englishman writing and thinking in the atmosphere that surrounded him and without any great desire to escape it.

If Chapman and Pope are the greatest examples of the translator who produces an 'original', the finest of those who have, consciously or unconsciously, tried to keep an ancient mind in a modern body is surely Dryden; a mere four lines from his Lucretius will show his power:

> What has this bugbear death to frighten man,
> If souls can die, as well as bodies can? . . .
> From sense of grief and pain we shall be free,
> We shall not feel, because we shall not be.

Homer, Virgil, Horace and Ovid have provoked the greatest number of translators, which is only to be expected; Catullus has brought more to grief than any other poet, which is likewise unremarkable, for translating Catullus is like singing Mozart – there is nowhere to hide. The more credit to Abraham Cowley, no great servant of the muses in his own right, for a delightful and almost wholly successful version of 'Acme and Septimius', which ends thus:

> If the Gods would please to be
> But advis'd for once by me,
> I'de advise 'em when they spie
> Any illustrious piety,
> To reward her, if it be she
> To reward him, if it be he;
> With such a husband, such a wife,
> With Acme's and Septimius' life.

I wish Mr Stoneman had included more versions of the same passages by different hands; we have Milton and Landor competing in one Horatian Ode, and Congreve and Allan Ramsay in another, but that is all. The Ramsay is an astonishing achievement, reminding me of Henley's dazzling success with Villon's 'Tout aux tavernes et aux filles', which he turned into the equivalent English thieves' argot ('Booze and the blowens cop the lot'); it is pure Burns, and in places needs another translation, but I finished it wanting to cheer:

> Guid claret best keeps out the cauld,
> An' drives awa' the winter soon;
> It makes a man baith gash an' bauld,
> An' heaves his saul ayont the moon . . .
>
> Her laugh will lead you to the place
> Where lies the happiness you want,
> An' plainly tells you to your face,
> Nineteen nay-says are hauf a grant.

Herrick at translation sounds almost more like Herrick than Herrick in his own voice; Johnson hardly comes to life; Bulwer-Lytton turns in a surprisingly good Horace; William Morris, anachronistic to the last, returns to the fourteener; the Browning Version, for all Mr Stoneman's defence of it, is terrible; Gladstone and Swinburne rub shoulders uneasily; I find more in Pound's translations than ever I have in his own work; Gilbert Murray survives all attempts (including Eliot's) to overthrow him.

Observer January 9th, 1983

The flavours of a lifetime

THE DEATH LAST week of John Stais closes more than a long and fruitful life. He was almost the last of a breed of restaurateurs who flourished, mainly in Soho, before the Second World War, and who survived to re-establish the old standards after it, and, in many cases, to go on for decades more. Their restaurants were not of the *grand luxe*, and they relied neither on glamour in the surroundings nor on inventiveness in the kitchen; they lived on consistency, and it was a mark of John Stais's quality that his staff stayed with him through the years; there are waiters at the White Tower who were there when I first started visiting it, more than twenty years ago, and they do not seem to have aged by a minute in all that time. (I trust they will be tactful enough to return the compliment.)

The same is true of the Etoile, just along the street from the White Tower, where the same head-waiter has been intoning the delights of the starters chariot in the same words ('. . marinated trout, a little sharp on the palate, *loup de mer* – sea-bass – with aïoli – garlic mayonnaise – or mayonnaise without garlic . . . '), and the same *sommelier* has been darting to and fro (I cannot remember ever seeing him walk), for a quarter of a century in my own memory alone. I began to eat at the Etoile when the amiable Mr Rossi was in charge. He passed it on to the no less genial Mr Vavlides, and the other day I saw a new and younger face at the table of the *patron*, and enquired whether the place had changed hands; only to be told, 'No, that's the guvnor's son.' (It is bad enough when the children of one's friends grow up, but when the new generation starts taking over in the restaurants something must be done, though unfortunately I cannot think what.)

L'Epicure has changed hands, though only after a reign of immense length by Michael and George (Michael was the tall, suave one and George was the short, twinkling one, or possibly the other way round), and I have been eating the *crevettes Alfonso* there since long before you were born, my dear, and when your mother was a mere gel. Maurer's has long since disappeared, though I can recall Madame, along with the gigantic portions she served, if I shut my eyes.

The late Isow's was always my favourite Jewish restaurant, first under the old man and then under his son, and there again the quality of the salt beef never varied from decade to decade. I used to lunch there alone when I felt like something substantial but not like company, and the hat-check lady mentioned this odd habit to a friend of mine a few days after I had had one of my solo meals. 'Funny,' she said, 'he doesn't even read a book.' Then she added words which I wouldn't mind as an epitaph: 'I suppose,' she said, 'he'd rather sit on his own than talk to fools.'

In a different category was the old Caprice (the fourth attempt, at least, to revive it is now under way, and I think this is the one that is going to be successful), but the Caprice had the greatest of all the *maîtres-d'hôtel* of my time: Mario, recognised and deferred to as *primus inter pares* by all his rivals.

Mario achieved the most extraordinary greeting ever addressed to me: 'Ah, Mr Levin,' he said 'you are just like Mr Gulbenkian.' I pointed out that I wore neither a beard nor a monocle, nor for that matter a lily in my button-hole, and I also hazarded a guess that I had less money than the celebrated Armenian. 'No, no,' said Mario, 'you both have a passion for plovers' eggs.' So indeed I did; Mario used to ring me up when the first ones appeared, and I would rush round and gorge upon them, frequently bumping into Gulbenkian in the door-way. Plovers' eggs are now *strengstens und polizeilich verboten*, though occasionally one turns up in a basket of gulls' eggs (they look very similar from the outside). I once complained about their banning, and got furious letters from ecology-prigs saying that I ought to be ashamed of myself. One of them even went so far as to say that a plover is considerably prettier than I am; very possibly, but I wouldn't eat as well.

And then there was Madame Prunier, where the *bisque* stayed the same to the end, and the *pot de chocolat à l'orange* was the best I have ever tasted; she was the perfect Parisienne, and I was always half persuaded that she had a fresh hair-do after every course she served.

Tempora mutantur . . . it is no use asking what has become of the Isola Bella, or Fava, or Canuto's (most of them, like most of Soho, are now strip-joints or massage-parlours), for the world will not stay still even for men well struck in years who wish it would. Mario and Franco represented the best of what replaced the old guard; they were, indeed, the modern equivalent in their heyday. But elsewhere, an entirely new race has arisen.

Today's typical restaurateurs, running today's typical restaurants, are polished diplomats – men like Richard Walton at Chez Moi or Mr Livingstone (I presume) of the English House, or Didier at the Brasserie St Quentin, or the Franco-Japanese team at the Bagatelle, where once, paying the bill, I pulled the candle towards me for better illuminating my fountain-pen, and the *patron* murmured in my ear, 'They say that cheques written by candlelight should only be cashed by moonlight.'

One of the new kind, and very recent, is quite the best establishment to be founded in London for much more than a decade, but it is so tiny that I dare not name it, lest I should ever after be unable to get a table for the crowds who have taken my advice. I must give clues, though: of the couple who own it, he is the nephew of an eminent British musician and she is the chef (she is entirely self-taught, and a friend I took there the other night wrote to ask, 'What do you suppose would happen if she started taking lessons?'); the establishment is named after their daughter; and the street it is to be found in (at no. 143) is probably the least likely thoroughfare in London, with the possible exception of the Balls Pond Road, to sport a restaurant of such remarkable quality.*

There is Nico Ladenis (Chez Nico), of course, who really does aim at perfection; visitors should be reassured that though he looks and sounds like a pirate, he is really a genial soul under the fierceness, and his cooking matches the beauty of his Dinah-Jane, more than which I can hardly say. Last time I was there he pointed in justifiable rage to a table laid for six; the party who had booked it had not turned up and not bothered to telephone their cancellation, while he had had to refuse other would-be diners.

John Stais presided with warmth and tact and unfailing skill and devotion over the White Tower: his great catch-phrase 'There's a duckling in the oven' will live as long as he lives in the memory of his friends, and that will be long indeed. I hope he feasts well with the angels, though their ambrosia, I feel sure, will not match his taramasalata.

But I said he was 'almost the last' of his kind; the very last of all is Victor Sassie, now grown perfectly spheric-

*Oh, all right; it is Mijanou.

134

al, still ruling the Gay Hussar, and still providing there the best value for money to be had at any restaurant in London. How he does it, I don't know, but I am very glad he does. Don't miss the wild cherry soup (it's the cherries that are wild, not the soup), and if there is a goose to be had, have it.

The Times   September 17th, 1983

More than a bowl of rice

CONTEMPLATING THE PRESENT discussion, in political circles and the press, of the future of Hongkong, I own to feeling very slightly sick. Wherever you cut the argument, it bleeds nothing but money; not only in the form of the alarming but hardly surprising decline in the value of the Hongkong dollar, knocked off its perch by the emergence from all the inevitable uncertainties of a growing conviction that the British government will sooner or later betray the people of the Crown Colony, but – much more powerful and effective in bringing on nausea – in the fact that the entire debate is couched in terms of Hongkong's *economic* future.

How can we ensure that, after the lease runs out in 1997, Hongkong will be able to continue making money in the manner to which it is accustomed? Do the authorities in Peking not realise that its economic stability and continuity are essential to them also, as it provides them with a very substantial part of their earnings of hard currency? What will happen to the free gold market? Whither Sir Run Run Shaw? Whence the funds for essential investment over the next few years? Whose little pigs are these, these, these, whose little pigs are these?

Has nobody noticed, or are we supposed to ignore in pursuit of an arrangement that will protect the divi-

dends of Jardine Matheson's shareholders, the fact that
there are five million human beings in Hongkong, who
are more important than the rate of exchange?

Somebody – probably the Foreign Secretary – will
soon say that fourteen years is a long time in politics,
meaning that if we all keep quiet the problem may go
away, that even if it doesn't we can start seeking a
solution to it about thirteen and a half years from now,
and that meanwhile nothing should be said or done that
might lead in Hongkong to further erosion of business
confidence. But the problem will not go away even if
we all sew our mouths shut with stout twine, so before I
go any further I may as well say what it is.

The internal constitutional arrangements of Hongkong are odd. It is one of the very few places which are
genuinely free without being democratic; that is, the
people do not elect their rulers, but they have genuine
freedom of speech, association, worship, publication
and the like (as well as economic freedom, in which
respect they are much more free than we are).

The non-material freedoms, as we may term them,
are not unlimited, as our own are not unlimited, and
clearly the extent of some of those freedoms among the
people of Hongkong is less than it is in Britain. Still,
their freedoms are real ones, they are of the same type as
ours and they are fully exercised. And it is these
freedoms that are at stake, and that if Hongkong reverts
to China will be extirpated.

'Extirpated' is an unminced word; but it is the right
one. The usual crowd of apologists for dictatorship have
been telling us for some years now that since the death
of Mao the rulers of China have become most frightfully democratic, but to know that that is a lie you have
only to notice that many of these apologists are the very
people who were insisting that Mao himself was frightfully democratic at the height of his Terror, and some
were saying before the Chinese Civil War ended that

137

Mao was not a communist at all, but an 'agrarian reformer'.

There is an apparently unbreakable rule that all communist dictators are criticised by their admirers, if at all, only after they have died or been replaced. While Stalin lived, he could do no wrong; when he died, it could safely be admitted that he had – well, gone a bit too far, in contrast with the liberal Khrushchev. Then Khrushchev was no more, and heads were shaken, lips pursed; thank goodness for the *truly* liberal Mr Brezhnev, who will have none of the excesses of his predecessor. Then Brezhnev died and was buried neatly, and at once we were being told that the almost unbearably liberal Mr Andropov was going to do away with the cruelties and oppressions of the brutal Brezhnev.

So it is with China. We have not, thank God, heard anything for some time from Messrs Felix Greene and Neville Maxwell; but look at the famous 'Wall of Democracy', with its array of hand-written posters and newspapers demanding elections and such. But you will need keen eyes to look at it; it was swept away a couple of years ago, and the writers of the messages shipped off to the concentr—— er, that is to say the *re-education* camps, in the Chinese interior, where they will have plenty of time to look forward to the denunciations of their jailers by Western fellow-travellers just as soon as their jailers have been replaced by new and unbelievably liberal successors.

If Hongkong reverts in 1997 to rule by China, it will be ruled by one of the most complete and ruthless dictatorships on earth. Not to be sure, the worst of all, and not with the insane ferocity of Mao's stormtroopers, but a system of government nevertheless that denies all the freedoms that we have in full in Britain and that the people of Hongkong have in ample measure. Fourteen years is *not* a long time in politics when the politics in question consists of matters as momentous as that.

Very well; he who pricks the bubble must provide the soap. If, as I insist, it is unthinkable that Britain should hand over five million British-protected persons, citizens of the Commonwealth for whom we have a direct and inescapable constitutional responsibility, to the monstrous tyranny of Chinese communism (as well as, incidentally, to the monstrous poverty of the same), what can and should be done about it while there is yet time?

First, let us agree that if the Chinese rulers stand upon their rights under the cession treaty, and it seems clear that they will, we cannot refuse to abide by its terms. It would be interesting, no doubt, to drop an independent nuclear deterrent or two on Peking, but that is not a practicable possibility, or for that matter a nice one. What other, more realistic, choices are there?

I believe that there is only one. We must regard Hongkong as a ship that is going to sink fourteen years from now, and we must mount a rescue operation to save *all* its passengers and crew. Those citizens of Hongkong who refuse to accept rule by China (no doubt some, not necessarily including all its substantial communist minority, will be willing to do so) must be helped to leave and to settle elsewhere.

Obviously, this cannot be done by simply inviting them to Britain, though as a matter of fact the astounding diligence, assiduousness and capacity for hard work that the Hongkong Chinese have displayed for many years could transform our economy. An abrupt influx of some millions of Asians would be unassimilable, quite apart from the clamour raised by Mr Enoch Powell, who, to judge by his comments on Lebanon, in any case probably believes that it is no business of Britain's who rules in Hongkong.

As soon as the question of the post-1997 rule of Hongkong is settled, Britain must launch what may well prove to be the most gigantic international enterprise ever conducted. Our government must not, of course, take the problem to the United Nations – as well hope to save a lamb from a tiger by putting it under the protection of a wolf – but must seek to set up and convene an association of countries willing to be part of the rescue operation. This means – must mean – willing to take in a share of the refugees; I know that this is not a propitious time to be asking countries struggling with recession to offer such hospitality, but we are entitled to demand that countries which value freedom for themselves should give *practical* help to the cause of freedom elsewhere; the American right, for a start, can show what sincerity there is in their eternal claim that US policy 'lost China to the communists' by demanding that their country play its full part in the operation. Nor can we be too squeamish about the invitations; just as the present Chinese totalitarianism is obviously not as bad as the Soviet one, so there are countries more or less authoritarian which for the refugees would be a very considerable improvement on rule from Peking, the most obvious of these being Singapore. (Taiwan, the natural choice, itself faces a too critical and uncertain future *vis-à-vis* China.)

On the whole, the modern world's behaviour towards refugees from tyranny has been appalling; from the persecuted Jews of Nazi Germany, via the victims of Yalta sent to their death in the Soviet Union at the end of the war, all the way to the 'boat people' of Vietnam, the characteristic sound of the West faced with appeals from the suffering has been the slamming of a door. Only India, who could hardly help herself in the circumstances, went against this sorry tide; a million people fled from East Bengal, or Bangladesh, into the already suffocating Calcutta. But Calcutta, it is worth pointing out, has survived.

In any case, the Hongkong refugees are different, in one crucial respect, from all others. Hitherto, refugees

have been those fleeing from tyranny, war, expropria-
tion or indeed natural catastrophe; but they have all been
fleeing from something actually happening to them, or
imminently about to. The rescue of the people of
Hongkong will be a rescue from something that is
inevitable, but is not due to happen for another fourteen
years. That means that, uniquely, there is time for the
help needed by the refugees to be carefully and gradually planned, explained, and finally provided.

But there will only be time for such an operation if it
is started *soon*. No doubt Mrs Thatcher wishes Hongkong had never existed, at any rate as a British responsibility. But it *is* a British responsibility, and if men must
die to uphold that responsibility in the South Atlantic,
they must live to uphold it in the China Sea.

Our government will be tempted to hope that something will turn up, to argue that the situation in a decade
or so may be utterly different from what it is now, even
to try the obvious fraud of accepting Chinese assurances
that Hongkong will be allowed to stay free. But the
earth goes round once a day, and when it has gone
round another 5,000 times or so, it will be too late to
turn it back. In the words with which Churchill used to
end his wartime minutes: Action this day.

The Times   September 30th, 1983

The diary of a somebody

The Diary of Samuel Pepys: Vol. 10, Companion, Vol. 11, Index edited by R. C. Latham and W. Matthews*

THE FIRST VOLUME of this monumental, complete and certainly final edition of Pepys appeared in 1970, with an optimistic note from the publishers saying that it would be completed 'over the course of the next few years'. The last instalment of the Diary proper arrived in 1976, but Jacob had to serve Laban for another seven years until, with these last two ancillary (but indispensable) volumes, the whole mighty edifice is complete; they were published last Wednesday, the Diarist's 350th birthday.

From the first blast of the trumpet, thirteen years ago, it has been apparent that this was to be one of the most remarkable and praiseworthy achievements of scholarship and publishing in modern, or indeed any, times. The late Professor Matthews was responsible mainly for the transcription, Mr Latham, who until last year was Pepys Librarian at Magdalene College, Cambridge, mainly for the commentary, Companion and Index, and a vast array of other scholars put themselves and their learning at the disposal of the principal editors.

*Bell and Hyman, 1983.

The two final volumes maintain the impeccable standards set in the nine earlier ones of the Diary itself. Take
the Index first. It is a huge compilation; 600 columns in
clear, well-spaced type, not as black as the Diary
volumes but perfectly legible, and not merely exhaustive but exhaustively detailed. I open it at random; here
is Sir Edward Nicholas, whose entry covers a mere nine
lines but is nevertheless broken down into

> gift from Sandwich . . . administers oath to P and
> Sandwich . . . orders Navy Board to produce papers
> for Vane's trial . . . replaced . . . his public spir-
> it . . . alluded to . . .

Now turn to an entry that was bound to be very
substantial: Health, say (Pepys was no hypochondriac,
but he paid close attention to his own health, and had
much to say about that of others). The entry is divided
into 'Health (illness/disease/condition)' and 'Health
(remedies/treatment)'. The first of these is divided into
fifty-one sub-sections headed in small capitals ('ABSCESS,
AGUE, ALLERGY, APOPLEXY, BACK-ACHE, BOILS
. . . SMALLPOX, SPRAINS, STONE, THRUSH, TOOTH-
ACHE, ULCER, VOMITING') and each of these contains
anything up to thirty topical headings; the second is split
still further, remedies and treatment being divided into
'MEDICINAL' ('BALSAM, CORDIAL, DIURETIC, ELECTU-
ARY, ENEMA . . . ') 'SURGICAL' ('AMPUTATIONS, CAUT-
ERY, DENTISTRY . . . '), 'DRESSINGS', 'DIET' and 'OTHER
TREATMENTS', each of these sub-sub-headings being in
turn further broken down topically.

I have tried every kind of trick question I could think
of on this astonishing guide to the Diary, and have not
been able to catch it out in a single *lacuna*; it even
enumerates completely, for those minded to seek them
all at one go, the occasions on which Pepys felt (usually,
though not invariably, because they recorded his sexual

adventures) that even his shorthand was not sufficiently impenetrable, and wrote the entries in a curious *lingua franca* of his own.

So much for the Index. The 600-page Companion volume comprises a vast biographical dictionary of every individual who pays any real part in the Diary, a gazetteer, a glossary (sixty two-column pages), and a comprehensive coverage of events, social conditions, theatres, taverns, history, books, institutions, religion, arts and customs; except for the glossary the volume is arranged in a single alphabetical sequence, and there are also maps, a chronology of the Diarist's life and an eight-generation genealogy.

But this volume is not just a vast opencast mine from which information may be wheeled away freely by the barrowload. Many of the more substantial entries are fascinating and valuable studies of their subjects. Take Music, for instance, which played a great part in Pepys's life and his Diary. Contributed by Dr Richard Luckett (who has succeeded Mr Latham as Pepys Librarian) the entry is a massive essay of some 13,000 words, ranging over the historical background, the styles, techniques and instruments of the period, the leading composers, systems of notation and gamut, and of course the Diarist's musical accomplishments, tastes and frustrations.

Just as good are the entries on The Navy and The Dutch Wars (both in the safe hands of Mr Richard Ollard, himself a devoted and expert Pepysian), the much-indexed Health (the Companion entry even includes 'A Psychoanalyst's View', contributed by Mr Martin Howard Stein), The Plague (one of the most interesting and informative in the book, contributed by Mr Christopher Morris), Food, which even includes some of Pepys's favourite recipes, and The Royal Society (Mr A. Rupert Hall). Compared with these, though, the entry on Charles II is disappointingly skimpy, and his brother James rates only a few lines more.

The immense quantity of learning in the Companion (most of the entries are by Mr Latham himself) is worn as lightly as in the Commentary to the Diary itself, which has been one of the most attractive features of the vast project. There are even some pleasantly donnish jokes, like the reference to the doctor who caught the plague but survived it, 'in spite of putting a dried toad on his chest when he felt the first symptoms'. But the standard of the scholarship that the jokes adorn never falls away in even the smallest detectable particular; the Index concludes with six pages of corrections of errors, from the nine volumes of the Diary proper, that have come to light since they were first published, and these not only include a rigorous listing of the few misprints, but go so far as to distinguish between 'Corrections', which have already been incorporated in the reprints that have been issued to meet the constant demand, and 'Corrigenda', which are those noted here for the first time.

It is worth remarking – indeed it is an obligation as well as a pleasure to remark – that the standard of physical production fully matches that of the editing. The typeface is a handsome, unassertive Bembo; the printers for the first nine volumes were Richard Clay (The Chaucer Press) Ltd of Bungay; they have also set these two in type, and Fletcher & Son of Norwich have printed them. The binding is a splendid dark green buckram with red title-pieces on the spine and Pepys's bookplate (a design of two anchors) embossed in gold on the front cover. *Finis coronat opus*; or as Mr Latham, off-duty at last, may surely be allowed to say: and so to bed.

Observer February 27th, 1983

Ars longa, Booker brevis

I THINK WE had better straighten out our ideas about literature, publication, book prizes and book promotion. There has of late been much high-minded comment about such enterprises as the '12 Best Post-War Novels' and the Booker prize; Mr Christopher Booker (no relation) was speaking for such views a few days ago when he wrote that:

> The publishing and bookselling trade has never been so geared to producing vast quantities of glossily packaged, frenetically publicized books, the great majority of which . . . are little more than rubbish . . . Most of those engaged in 'the book business' have been swept up into a self-deluding charade which has . . . little to do with the real merits of literature . . .

At the same time Mr Nicholas de Jongh, taking a welcome break from his normal weekly announcement that the Royal Shakespeare Company is about to close down for lack of funds, devoted himself to a theme nowadays heard at least as frequently as Mr Booker's; he declared that the Arts Council's Literature Department, Marghanita Laski up, has failed the nation and must go, adducing as his evidence that:

There could be no more damning testimony to the literature department's creative bankruptcy than the fact that for the last two financial years . . . the department failed to spend a considerable portion of its grant allocation . . . In the last two years it has focused attention on the encouragement of readers rather than writers . . .

On the face of it, the argument espoused by the high-minded Booker (who writes on vellum in an unheated monk's cell with a signed photograph of Aristotle on the wall before him) is the very opposite of that put forward by the low-minded de Jongh (who writes at Langan's Brasserie on a word-processor lightly sprinkled with Beaujolais Nouveau). The one is appalled at the publication and boosting of 'non-books by non-authors'; the other is so eager for more authors to get their bread in the gravy that he condemns the Arts Council for withholding bursaries from the authors of 'indifferent work' – presumably Booker's 'non-books by non-authors'. Booker condemns the 'seedy mediocrity' of his namesake prize, and deplores the 'huge, fraudulent structure' of the publicity machine; de Jongh calls for a Literature Trust to 'seek out serious writers far more successfully than the Literature Department has managed' – no doubt with the aid of Booker's 'huge, fraudulent structure' – and denounces the 'lofty elitists' who have neglected such essential seeking, presumably with the applause of Booker.

Yet it seems to me that both of these critics of the present state of affairs are trapped in the same fallacy. They assume that literature is a plant as frail and endangered as the darling buds of May and that it can flourish only if the right conditions – more money in de Jongh's view, less vulgarity in Booker's – are present; they also believe that whatever the right conditions are they can be brought into being by the actions of the right people.

When the Decca Record Company made its historic first recording of *The Ring*, the BBC in turn made a television programme about its making. *The Songwriters' Guild News* protested at the lavishing of such resources on such a work, and asked indignantly: 'Can the BBC find no British work of comparable stature to film? If not, surely they could have commissioned one.'

To be sure, that is a somewhat extreme form of missing the point, but in principle the writer was doing the same as Messrs Booker and de Jongh (and for that matter Fay Weldon, whose speech at the Booker Prize award dinner managed to combine both of their approaches). For you see, a publisher – or a Literature Trust, or an Arts Council, or for that matter a committee of angels presided over jointly by Shakespeare, Homer and Tolstoy – can draw up a book contract for an author to sign, so scrupulously and tightly drafted that it binds him inescapably to produce, under the most fearsome penalties, a book of the required subject and the required length at the required time; they can make sure that he will not dare to spend the advance on fast women and slow horses; they can insist that they monitor his progress chapter by chapter; they can demand that he provides photographs, diagrams and an index at his own expense; they can leave him in no doubt that if the book results in a libel action they will hold him responsible for all damages and costs; but in this world, and I suspect in the next also, no enforceable contract can contain, even as a sub-clause of a sub-section of a sub-heading, any guarantee that the book, when delivered, will be found to be a masterpiece.

One view holds that unless writers are given more of other people's money literature will die out; the other states that unless writers are given less of other people's noise the same unhappy fate will befall the art. The proponents of the first view cannot accept that the quality of the writing should be the test for a handout ('The contraction in the number of bursaries – on the ground that too much indifferent work had been supported – may have been a tactical mistake'); the advocates of the second welcome the suspicion that the self-publicising shrewdness of the Booker Prize donors has backfired ('the sole beneficiaries of their generosity [are] a handful of rapacious publishers and their lucky authors').

I do not believe that any true work of literature will come out of any scheme of public grants to authors, which would otherwise never have been written; nor do I believe that any scheme of private prizes to unworthy recipients will inhibit any worthy but disappointed writer from producing a true work of literature if that is what he has in him. The often-made analogy with opera and drama is false; for the performance arts hundreds of people are required, with complex relationships and valuable time, and in modern conditions these often cannot be provided at unsubsidised cost. But for a book, all that is required is one man or one woman, equipped with one pencil and one packet of paper.

That simple combination will not be irreparably broken by the sound and fury of the literary circus, nor will it be in the least affected by the production of non-books by non-authors. Neither Harold Robbins nor Marghanita Laski, neither 'the books business' nor the 'lofty elitists', have any power to harm or to create literature, which has never been, cannot be, and never will be, created by anything but the interaction of a single mind and a single soul.

'What is art', asked Samuel Butler, 'that it should have a sake?' We might well ask, and it is not nearly so easy to find an answer as it should be. I rely instead on the Sieve of History. Chatterton died of poverty, but his work lives; Marie Corelli died of diamonds, but hers does not. On the other hand, Thomas Mann was a genius and made a lot of money from his books; the ninety-fifth imitation of *The Day of the Jackal* was neither better nor worse than the original, and was remaindered a fortnight after publication. I tell you that justice does rule the world, and books are not exempt from its judgements, eccentric or capricious though these sometimes seem.

I do not object to the giving of modest sums, provided out of our taxes, to authors considered fitted to receive them. Nor do I object to the giving of huge sums, provided by commercial sponsors, to authors plainly unfitted to receive anything but cries of derision. But the cause of literature will be neither advanced nor set back by either. Mr Booker and Mr de Jongh will stay in after school and write out one hundred times: 'Shakespeare said "Not marble, nor the gilded monuments Of princes, shall outlive this powerful rhyme", and Shakespeare was right.'

The Times November 15th, 1983

A Ring *for all* *seasons*

A T ABOUT SEVEN o'clock in the evening on Monday of last week, in the middle of Act II of *Die Walküre*, Hildegarde Behrens embarked upon the long dialogue in which she brings the tidings of death to the doomed hero, with the words 'Siegmund, sieh auf mich' ('Siegmund, look on me'). At that moment, a puff of white smoke was seen to emerge from the *Festspielhaus* chimney, and the vast throng on the terrace, many of whom had been there, patiently awaiting this moment, for anything up to thirty years, fell to their knees; some were openly weeping, and a few of the more elderly ones, mostly French, expired on the spot, their faces wreathed in beatific smiles. Then the Cardinal-Secretary, Herr Wolfgang Wagner, stepped on to the balcony over the main entrance, gave the traditional blessing, *Urbe et orbi*, and pronounced the fateful words, so long unheard in these parts: 'Habemus Brünnhildam'.

All we need now is a Wotan and a Siegfried, and we shall have the fixings of an uncommonly fine *Ring*.

I paused in Salzburg for a few days en route, to lay in some Mozart, like a man hastily putting on a thick pullover when the pilot announces that all the engines have failed and the aircraft is going to ditch in the sea. I was greeted, alas, by a sign that the world is coming to an end even more rapidly than I had supposed; a McDonald's in the Getreidegasse, almost bang opposite the front door of the Goldener Hirsch. No matter; there was also a *Così Fan Tutte*, lovingly and lingeringly conducted by Muti, with Bruscantini as Alfonso and the finest Mozart tenor singing I have ever heard in my life, from Francesco Araiza. Then I donned my sandals and my habit of coarse woollen cloth roughly tied with string, put a crust of bread and a few radishes in my scrip, took my staff in hand, and set off on my quinquennial pilgrimage to the holy place of Wagner, to sit in terrible darkness for sixteen hours and there experience once more the effect of this unique music-drama, which bites its victims more deeply than any other work of art I know, and bites them, moreover, with teeth coated in a strange hallucinatory drug which induces a condition well described by the Ancient in Shaw's *Back to Methusaleh*: 'Infant! one moment of the ecstasy of life as we live it would strike you dead.'

Why do we do it? Certainly not to enjoy the delights of Bayreuth, a notoriously undelightful town. (It, too, has a McDonald's, but here it is hardly out of place, for there has been a Parsifal Chemist's in the High Street for at least a quarter of a century, and what I paid for a cummerbund would have kept Wagner in quilted silk dressing-gowns for at least twice as long.) All sensible folk shun Bayreuth entirely, and stay out at Pegnitz with the good Herr Pflaum, whose hotel, now a member of the Relais et Châteaux confraternity, is better run and more comfortable than ever (I have an apartment so enormous that in addition to an ordinary bathroom it sports a jacuzzi pool in solid onyx that takes me ten minutes to wade across), with Brother Hermann in the kitchen muttering spells, to good effect, over the *zicklein knusprig gebraten*, and a young waitress the living image of Maggie Smith.

Why do we do it? Whatever the answer, we are in good company. From where I stand, waiting for the fanfare to summon us back to our seats and wondering whether I have time for another brace of sausages before the interval ends, I can see, among the British contingent alone, a former Prime Minister, a Secretary to the Cabinet, a former Minister of the Arts, a former chairman of Covent Garden, a royal duke, a Warden of Wadham, a genius, a saviour of Venice, a young composer on his honeymoon, a young barrister on hers (the same one, actually), a director-general, and a man who claims to have acquired a ticket for *Götterdämmerung* this very morning by mingling with the seething crowd outside the box office (sold out since last November) in search of what he called 'the most obviously criminal face I could spot' and, when he spotted it, asking it out of the corner of his mouth whether it had one of the precious pieces of cardboard to sell at double the official price, being instantly rewarded for both his ingenuity and his perspicacity by discovering that he had hit, first go, upon the leading ticket-tout of the Bayreuth Festival, if not of all Bavaria.

But why do we do it? This year, at any rate, there is an extra answer. When Georg Solti and Peter Hall (they are known as '*die Sirs*' in the town) were engaged for the new Bayreuth *Ring*, they promised that they, together with Hall's chosen designer, William Dudley, would give Wagner everything he asked for in the stage directions – settings, supernumeraries and all. ('Even a bear?' I asked Sir Peter incredulously when I heard of this rash promise. 'Even a bear,' he replied with hardly a tremor in his voice. And there it is, in Act I of *Siegfried*, large, brown and furry, and plainly longing to growl.) Now a naturalistic *Ring* has been long overdue; I have not seen the door of Hunding's parlour fly open to admit the moonlight since the late 1940s, and I doubt if Fricka's chariot has been drawn by rams since Wagner

153

died. Well, in this *Ring* the door flies open and the moonlight floods the stage as it floods the orchestra, and when Fricka arrives in the next Act she arrives, as Wagner specifies, in a chariot drawn by rams, and very handsome black rams they are, too.

That is by no means all. The forest scenes are beautifully set and staged, their trees like the real trees I see on my way in to Bayreuth on board Herr Pflaum's festival bus, and the sunlight, falling through their branches, perfectly convincing, as are most of the interiors – Mime's smithy, for instance, and Nibelheim, where Alberich has built himself a golden throne. There is a real rope for the Norns, too, real water for the Rhinemaidens (stark naked, incidentally, though one of them needs to take her bottom to the sunshine on some secluded beach, for at present it is disconcertingly paler than the rest of her) and a truly savage dragon, looking like a cross between a Siberian mammoth and a science-fiction giant lobster. I swear that there are even real flames on the stage for the Immolation, in which case some of the Gibichungs milling around the pyre had better be firemen in disguise.

Nor is it just a matter of authentic props and scene-painting; the movement, especially for the Rhine-maidens and the Vassals, is as good as anything I have ever seen on an operatic stage, and the great set-pieces – notably the Entry into Valhalla and the Funeral March – are replete with imagination and integrity, as indeed are many of the details, such as the dinosaur into which Alberich turns himself in the first transformation instead of the usual snake or dragon (inevitably upstaged later by the real dragon), and the murder of Fasolt by his brother, accomplished not with a club but with a chunk of the fatal gold. The acting, it is true, is mostly no more than a sketch so far, and in some cases hardly even that, but the obvious intentions behind the sketch offer hope for a finished picture next year or the year after.

There are mistakes, of course, the worst of them being Hall's decision to use a gauze, which fuzzes everything, particularly that which should not be fuzzed. Then again, the Valkyries' collection of the bodies from the battlefield is a mess, and the Gibichung Hall, until the final scene, is horribly cramped, besides being carpeted, apparently, in bird-droppings.

Yet a *Ring* cannot be made out of authenticity alone. Peter Hall's success lies in the way he has enabled us, by his fidelity to the wishes of a composer with a well-deserved reputation for knowing his own mind, to see both the drama and its meanings plain. Away with the 'interpretations' we have had these last years, mostly by salon-Marxists who have never read more than two paragraphs of Marx and understood neither. Away with the incessant hunger to *épater les bourgeois*, to draw parallels that are not parallel and conclusions that conclude nothing. Away with everything that blocks our path into the heart of Wagner's mystery with signposts that claim to be directing us there.

Wagner's great tale of will and power, of love, renunciation and redemption, of sacrifice and self-sacrifice, will speak clearly enough to an audience when the director has the courage – as Hall has had – to let it do so, to seek the truth in the relationships, in the characters and their natures, in the symbolism, in the struggle of strength that cannot be waged through force ('Nichts durch Gewalt!'), in the Shakespearian understanding of the human heart that runs right through this most heroic of dramas. (No director who does not comprehend Shakespeare can succeed in the *Ring*, and Hall is one of our finest Shakespearian directors.) The clue lies in the pattern of the *leitmotifs*; these will always guide us to the meanings, great and small, and it is a measure of Hall's success that I cannot remember having seen or heard a *Ring* in which they made Wagner's points, with all their complexity and many-sidedness, in a manner at once so urgent, so clear and so illuminating.

But why, I ask yet again, do we do it? Why do we put up with the discomfort, the expense, the monomania all round us, the frightful drivel in the programme-book (this year's coveted Gibberish Prize was won effortlessly by Claude Lévi-Strauss – how did that man acquire a reputation even in our gullible age?), the monstrous demands made upon our time and attention?

We do it for the music, on which we are drunk, hopelessly drunk, from the first intimation of the Rhine as the E flat steals out into the darkness to the final moment, a week later, as the Redemption theme spreads its healing wings in benediction over a world made anew by love.

So far I have concentrated on Peter Hall's direction and William Dudley's settings. Now I must hail Solti's triumph in the pit. (A pit indeed; during the *Siegfried* of the first cycle, the temperature beneath the wooden shell that covers the orchestra touched 111 degrees.) Disaster is inevitable in all productions of Wagner; there is no such thing as an understudy, because if you can remember some of the words and sing most of the notes in more or less the right key you can write your own contract anywhere in the world, and this production was horribly beset. From the new Siegfried, Rainer Goldberg, much was expected; he was said to have the true *Heldentenor* voice, and had been preparing for his ordeal for nearly three years. Alas, at the final, public, dress rehearsal he went to pieces, and had to be replaced by Manfred Jung. The trouble with Jung is the same as the trouble with Siegmund Nimsgern, the chosen Wotan; we know the furthest inch of which they are capable, and there was no chance that either would astound us, as Hildegarde Behrens did with her Brünn-hilde. So the search continues for the two other legs of the tripod on which every *Ring* must stand, and it is a measure of the plight in which Wagner conductors live that among the names being bandied about for Siegfried was Placido Domingo; why, if I had offered to sing the part myself I could have found a dozen people willing to put me on their list before the end of the interval.

In addition to Behrens, who sang with an amplitude and beauty of tone that made it difficult to believe that this was her first *Ring*, there were only two really outstanding voices: Aage Haugland as Hagen and Jeannine Altmeyer as Sieglinde, *proxime accessit* for a future Brünnhilde herself. Not enough; all now rested on Solti's shoulders.

His reading was fast (at the end of Act I of *Götterdämmerung* I thought my watch must have stopped, for he took only one hour and fifty minutes, which may be a record), yet although it was full of intensity and force it never seemed hurried, so perfectly paced was it. The spring of nervous energy in Solti's Wagner is now completely flexible, a servant not a master, and the consequence is that it is impossible to imagine better conducting in the *Ring* than he has given us here, or for that matter better playing than he succeeded in drawing from the invisible orchestra.

The climaxes surged forth in all their splendour – the end of *Rheingold*, the *Ride*, the *Götterdämmerung* chorus, Waltraute's flight to her lost sister, the duel, the forging of the sword, the murder of Siegfried – but they never seemed, as they so often do, like separate bits of washing on a line; the great span of Solti's conception held everything in place, everything balanced, everything organic. And he knew when to slow down; the invocation to the unborn hero as Wotan leaves the fire was echoed by the trombones with majestic deliberation, and 'Ruhe, Ruhe, du Gott' was like the placing in position of the final stone of a tomb.

It is impossible, I know, to convince anyone who does not love Wagner's music that it is lovable; either you feel that when you hear it, or it is not for you. I travelled to Salzburg with my friend Count Alois von Vorsicht-Stufe, for instance; the Count is a passionate and profoundly knowledgeable Mozartian, but he declined all suggestions that he should come on to Bayreuth with me. To change his mind, I played him a bit on the way; he listened attentively for about a quarter of an hour, then said in measured tones, 'It's all very interesting, but when does the music start?' It is useless to talk, in these circumstances, of the unbroken thread of melody, of the orchestra as the chief voice, of the way in which the themes are continuously transformed; we know what secret it is that the others do not share. I told the Count, when he begged me to explain to him just what it was that I got out of Wagner, that it was as though every bit of my mind, my body, my psyche and my soul had been unscrewed, sand-blasted, polished for thirty-six hours, bathed in the most expensive *eau de cologne*, put together again and gift-wrapped, knowing all the while that those who have not experienced it will not understand, and those who have experienced it will not need to understand. And very rarely indeed have I felt the experience as I just have in Bayreuth.

The greatest coup was in the final bars of *Die Walküre*. For Act III, Hall and Dudley had reverted to the tilting platform that has unfortunately become standard for productions of the *Ring* in recent years. (The Valkyrie sisters had to be anchored when it swung vertically, and Brünnhilde, poor girl, was at one point strapped upside-down beneath it, waiting – for two and a half minutes – until it turned right over and allowed her to get her circulation back.) When the platform first appeared, a groan of protest seemed in order, but it was stifled on my lips, and indeed I was unable to make a sound of any kind, by what happened just before the curtain fell.

Wotan has laid his beloved, erring daughter to rest,

and summoned Loge to guard her with fire. The ring of red is unbroken around her, and the flames that dim night's candles in the velvet darkness above her are depicted in the music, barring the way to all but the fearless hero who is to awaken her. Wotan, with infinite, resigned pity and regret, strides out of the magic circle and out of the scene. And at that moment the whole platform, with the sleeping heroine clad in her finery of fire, took off like some great space-ship, and went sailing up the sky so that she might sleep, fittingly, among the stars. I knew then the quality of this *Ring* for all seasons, and I knew also exactly why we who love the work do so.

The Times   August 16th–17th, 1983

Love and flotsam

A Durable Fire: The letters of Diana and Duff Cooper 1913-1950
edited by Artemis Cooper*

AFTER HER OWN three volumes of memoirs and the biography by Philip Ziegler, is there any more to be said about the life of Lady Diana Cooper, *recte* the Dowager Lady Norwich?

Absurd question! To start with, that silver tongue is not silent yet, and will not be, I trust, until she has buried the rest of us; from the tear she lets fall on my own grave I shall expect lilies of the valley, at the very least, to spring. Moreover, for those of us who love her but never knew her husband (he died thirty years ago), Duff Cooper is a figure glimpsed through a doorway; of the magnitude of her love for him there can be no doubt, but the quality of the man who inspired it has hitherto eluded those who seek him. (His own autobiography, *Old Men Forget*, is a wooden affair.)

Here comes Diana's granddaughter to let us eavesdrop as he speaks directly to his wife, and she to him. It seems that each kept all the other's letters; this volume includes about a quarter of the total. The editing is admirably skilled; the work must have posed formid-

*Collins, 1983.

160

able problems, chiefly in the matter of sorting out the gigantic cast that flits through the pages. Miss Cooper has here erred on the side of comprehensiveness, and offers footnote identifications of, among others, Baldwin, Chaliapin, D'Annunzio ('the Italian poet'), Lady Astor and Eisenhower.

She is also exceptionally assiduous in ascribing, and where necessary correcting, the quotations with which both correspondents fill their letters, though the sacred rule which lays down that a reviewer must show himself to be, in at least one respect, cleverer than the book, obliges me to point out that she has missed a Shakespearian line on page 228 and another on page 231.

When the letters begin, Diana is twenty-one and breaking hearts with the insouciance, rapidity and copiousness that others bring to the shelling of peas. A Bright Young Thing before the species officially existed (morphia then played the role in fashionable society now occupied by cocaine), she at first plainly regarded Duff as only another beau to her string, while he wore his heart upon his sleeve for her to peck at. It was not long, however, before she knew she had met her match:

> My darling love, I can think only of you and of your beauty and sereneness to me, and of all my extravagent [*sic*] dreams and demands that you have fulfiled [*sic*]. I adored your glorious spirits . . . I am terrified that I clung and clamoured about you too much . . . Many of my tears were sheer love unmixed with pity and desolation. I loved to feel them fall and feel the strong tide of love within me.

(The *sics* are mine; the book's editor eschews their use – wisely, or there would scarcely be a page without a dozen, for Diana's spelling has always had a life of its own, its high point in this volume being her reference to 'the whiches of Salem'.)

The mask was finally laid away when Duff went to the war; he had not been allowed to enlist earlier, because of his job in the Foreign Office, but he was at the front in April 1918, and distinguished himself repeatedly in action, while she trembled in terror at every casualty list (she was working in London as a nurse, among conditions which belied the frivolous image), and he whistled in the dark to keep her spirits up:

> You surely, darling, have never doubted how madly proud and wildly happy I should always have been and always will be to marry you under any conceivable conditions, how little I should mind poverty, how gladly I should renounce all my extravagances and vices, break my champagne glasses, throw away my cigars, tear up my cards, sell all my books, the first editions first, study the habits of buses and the intricacies of tubes to obtain that inconceivable honour. You don't believe this – you shake your lovely head, your pale eyes look reproaches for past transgressions and too recent ones but, oh my best, you can surely see how different it would all be then.

That combination of love and wit is to be found on both sides, and is the most attractive and enriching feature of the book, though not all the letters included are of such a nature, and at times the lone and level sands stretch far away, with never an oasis in sight. One of the problems is the world that first Diana, then both of them, moved in, heavily populated as it was with people of no significance at the time, let alone now, and as I waded through Luffy and Poppy and Bongy and Denny and Vinny and Maudi and Dickie and Hutchy and Holly and Fairy and Pinchie and Letty and Dolly and Nannie and Biddy and Geordie and Cardie, followed by Poots and Chips and Crooks and Oc and Van and Buck and Oom and Bee and Val and Glad and Sid and Fish and Trim, to say nothing of Buffles and Scatters and Kakoo and Puffin and Kaetchen and Duckling and Donkey and Bobbety, I began to long for Robespierre to make a dramatic entrance carrying a small but serviceable guillotine.

Between the love and the flotsam there are some fascinating sidelights on history; Diana's year-long *succès fou* in *The Miracle* gives rise to some wonderful accounts of the bitching and scratching that went on backstage, and the Duff's-eye-view of appeasement and later, of de Gaulle, brings the familiar past to vivid life. And it is nice to see Oswald Mosley summed up (by Duff) long before he became a Fascist, indeed while he was still the rising star of the Labour Party, as an 'adulterous, canting, slimy, slobbering Bolshie'.

Diana Cooper was born, like Shakespeare's Beatrice, under a dancing star. It has not waned yet, and when it does we shall have words, by which to remember it, like these:

I read a letter from you tonight – a veiled adieu, and cried a drenching patch on Alan's shoulder. He shall not have my letters. No one must know me as you have and shall. It is I that must edit them, and if I must be old it is I that shall read them to the envious young – flauntingly, exultantly – and when they hear yours they'll dream well that night, and waking crave for such a mythical supreme lover and regret that they are born in the wrong age – as once I did before I saw your light, crying for Gods and wooers.

Observer September, 18th, 1983

Who's right now?

OTHER COMMENTATORS HAVE discussed the Bermondsey by-election in terms of swings and tactical voting, the odds against an early General Election, or the effect of the opinion polls.

But it is another, more tangential aspect of the by-election that I want to dwell upon today; in fact it is so tangential that it can hardly be said to be connected with the contest at all. But it has a moral for us, if we will only heed it.

In the course of the campaign, there was a feature in the *Guardian* about the 'fringe' candidates, and one remark in it caused me to put down my coffee cup and sit staring out of the window for quite a long time. Of the Dowager Lady Birdwood, standing as an Independent Patriot (few, I think, will doubt that she is both), the writer said that she could 'at least boast a long pedigree in protest movements of the extreme right, starting with her crusade against *Oh! Calcutta!*'

Now Lady Birdwood's political opinions, so far as I understand them, are certainly to be found at the right-hand edge of the political spectrum, and indeed if they went much further in that direction she would be in danger of falling off. But the writer of the article to which I have referred took her political views for granted, and epitomized them with a single example;

her involvement in politics of 'the extreme right' began 'with her crusade against *Oh! Calcutta!'*

I think I may have the right to claim the credit for coining the term 'political Doppler shift', a few years ago, to denote a political phenomenon analogous to the scientific principle thus named. In this instance, Lady Birdwood seems to have fallen victim to the shift in a fairly spectacular manner, for we are now invited to believe that to oppose with vigour a sexually explicit nude stage show *in itself* reveals a political position on 'the extreme right'.

As the stuttering water-diviner said: 'Well, well, *well.*' I have no great interest in 'soft porn' (which is what for simplicity's sake we may call the performance in question), but have no wish at all to see such things banned or censored. On the other hand, we must have come a long way in a short time if trying to close down sex shows is *prima facie* evidence of a tendency to impose martial law and mutter 'Heil Hitler' in an absent-minded manner.

There is, as it happens, a delightful irony in this situation which escaped the writer of the article; many feminist groups today, some of them most certainly on the extreme left, oppose pornography and pornographic performances more vehemently than any Dowager, arguing that such material debases and degrades women, and even that it encourages violence against them. But pleasant though it would be to see the writer lynched on – and indeed by – the Women's Page of the *Guardian*, it is the Doppler shift that interests me today.

Who moved the marker? How were the terms of the debate rigged so that the centre was shifted three-quarters of the way along the spectrum to the left? You can see the effects directly in political discussion: Sir Keith Joseph, probably the gentlest, most unworldly and least fanatical British politician since George Lansbury, is widely believed, and not only by his more excitable political opponents, to dress up as Attila the Hun when he goes home at night, while Mr Jim Mortimer, general secretary of the Labour Party, who gets all misty-eyed at the thought of the Russian Revolution and the advances it brought to mankind, is a 'moderate'.

This is not just a matter of relativity, although it is often portrayed as such. Obviously, compared with the Labour fellow-travellers and Trotskyites, Mr Mortimer *is* a moderate, but it is not the comparison that establishes him as one; it is the fact that the very word 'moderate' now embraces anybody on the left who does not want to abolish Parliament, suppress the newspapers, invite the IRA to rule Northern Ireland and initiate the accession of Britain to the Warsaw Pact.

And, as the case of Lady Birdwood shows, it is not only in party or parliamentary activities that the shift has taken place. The right, even the extreme right, is now anybody with social, legal, educational, scientific, moral and even religious views less 'progressive' than those of say, *New Society*, Penguin Books, the management of the Royal Court Theatre, Professors Tessa Blackstone and Peter Townsend, Mr Des Wilson, the BBC Drama department, Mr Geoffrey Robertson, the National Council for Civil Liberties, Mr Clive James, Mr John Alderson, Dr John Rae, the Brook Advisory Centre, Lord Justice Scarman, the Glasgow University Media Studies Group, Miss Polly Toynbee, the Friends of the Earth, the Reverend Paul Oestreicher and Mr Salman Rushdie.

This cannot be healthy for our society, particularly since the process of moving the marker is a continuous one; five years from now, half a dozen of the individuals and institutions on my list will be officially classed as reactionaries, and ten years after that the whole lot of them will be described as being on 'the extreme right'. It was not, after all, in our great-grandfathers' time that

Mr John Osborne, Mr Christopher Logue and Mr Arnold Wesker were regarded as the avatars of British culture by the entire ranks of the left, and now those ranks regard them with suspicion and hostility, and will shortly excommunicate them altogether. Yet Messrs Osborne, Logue and Wesker have not changed their fundamental sympathies; it is the spectrum that has shifted.

I do not suppose it can be shifted back. But at any rate we can start to draw attention to the effects of the phenomenon I have described, and to insist that it does not ineluctably follow that a man who supports NATO, does not wish to read *Tribune* whoever runs it and regrets the destruction of the grammar schools must be a paid-up member of the Waffen SS with a private concentration camp in his back garden. Lady Birdwood undoubtedly has very right-wing views. But they cannot be deduced from the fact that she opposed the showing of *Oh! Calcutta!*

The Times February 28th, 1983

The roll-call of the dead

ABAKOKS BIRUTA, ABAKUKS ALEKSANDR, Abarios Emilja, Abats Janis, Abele Alfons, Abele Alma (son Edgar, son Edvin, son Valentin), Abele Artur, Abele Arvid, Abele Arvid, Abele Arvid, Abele Edgar, Abele Elvira, Abele Ernest, Abele Ernest, Abele Fricis, Abele Janis, Abele Janis, Abele Karl Konrad, Abele Liba, Abele Mikelis, Abele Mikelis, Abele Rudolf, Abele Sofia, Abele Rudolf Ernest, Abele Teodor, Abele Talivald Jekob . . .

Thus begins (and thus goes on for 677 pages) a book which I have just been sent; it contains nothing but a brief introduction and a list of names, from the very first page of which it will be apparent that 'Abele' is a very common surname somewhere. So indeed it is, in Latvia, for these are all Latvian names, and the book is published by the Latvian National Foundation in Stockholm.

And what, you may ask, am I doing reviewing the Swedish edition of the Latvian telephone directory? Has the heat finally got to my brain, or is this some merry jest? Alas, no; any man with the smallest imagination, as he turns the pages of this extraordinary volume, could be pardoned for wishing that he *had* gone mad, nor is there anything funny about it.

. . . Grodskis Eduard, Grodskis Ignats, Grodskis Jadviga (son Romald, daughter Regina), Grolmusi Erik Ernest, Gromolts Gerhard, Gromovs Aleksandra, Gromovs Anastasia, Gromovs Apolonis, Gromovs Janis, Gromovs Jekab, Gromovs Lazar, Groms Peter, Gromulds Gerhard, Gromulds Natalija, Grosbards Jekab, Grosbergs Albert . . .

Very well, what *is* all this about? If the title of the book, *These Names Accuse*, is not enough, the first paragraph of the prefatory matter will provide the answer for those with the slightest knowledge of the history of our tormented time:

> This book is a list of names. It is also an endless grey line of prisoners, forced to march through the streets of a conquered city. Those who did not share their fate should stop for a moment on the sidewalk of history and watch them pass by. Can you feel compassion towards this faceless grey multitude? Or does your compassion arise only when you look at another human face and think – it could have been me, they could have taken me, they might take me to march in these lines of prisoners?

The entries in the book, each of which is meticulously accompanied by its owner's last known address, number some 30,000, which represents roughly 5 per cent of what would be the total if complete records were available. These 30,000, the 'faceless grey multitude', are those Latvians known to have been deported, after the Soviet Union's seizure of their country in 1941, to the death-camps of Siberia; further mass culling took place in 1945, 1946 and 1949, and the arrests have continued, in smaller numbers, ever since (the most recent to be included in the catalogue was seized in 1978).

The more recent Baltic States victims have included some dissidents, those heroic souls who have been engaged in the struggle to prise loose their country from the grip of the cruellest imperialism the world has ever seen, amid the unbroken silence of the United Nations Committee on colonialism and of those in this country who are most vociferous in denouncing the neo-colonialism of the multi-national companies. But the original mass roundups were of a different character.

Stalin rightly understood that any resistance to tyranny, or at any rate any resistance wider than the actions of a few brave men and women which offer only a moral example, needs leaders; he reasoned, no less correctly, that in societies as homogeneous and patriotic as the Baltic States leadership could at first only come from those already prominent and respected in their communities; clergymen, doctors, businessmen, lawyers, army and police officers, teachers. So he concluded that if he took away and murdered as many of such people as could be found, the problem of resistance to his invasion and occupation of the Baltic States would be solved. As it happened, he was only partly right, for the armed struggle continued until the 1950s, and the nationalist and independence movements ultimately arose in Latvia, Lithuania and Estonia anyway; but obviously the extermination of so many potential opponents to Soviet rule must have weakened and delayed any form of opposition for many years.

. . . Mundeciems Gunar, Munderovskis Valter, Mundiciems Juris, Muduris Viktor, Munkevics Fricis, Munkevics Janis Visvaldis, Munkevics Karlis, Mukons Kazimir, Munters Vilis, Murans Aleksandr, Murans Aleksandr, Murans Edvard, Murans Vladislav, Muraska Karl, Murasko Peter, Murasko Vladislav . . .

I am myself of Lithuanian descent, from my father; this much-abbreviated Latvian list contains two Levins, and no doubt when the Lithuanian equivalent is compiled there will be some on that, too; perhaps I had uncles or cousins in Stalin's Holocaust. But I do not think it is necessary to be related to evil's victims in order to protest against it, and I am quite sure that it is unnecessary to have a blood-tie with an innocent martyr in order to feel a bond of sympathy with a fellow human done foully to death.

Ours is the day of the genocide, from Hitler and the Jews to Sinhalese and Tamils, via an apparently endless list of examples, involving greater or lesser numbers, in between. Stalin's slaughter of the captive peoples of the Soviet Empire (Robert Conquest has provided the best brief account of this tragic story in his *The Nation-Killers*) is among the most dreadful, but there was more logic to it than to Hitler's Final Solution or the Hindu-Moslem and Moslem-Hindu massacres that followed independence for the sub-continent in 1947, and all Stalin's successors, though the mass exterminations no longer take place, have seen the same point and enforced it ruthlessly.

. . . Trapans Anna (son Haris), Trapans Edgar, Trapins Anton, Trapsa Eduard, Trapsa Julianna, Trapsa Zinaida (son Peter, son Vladislav, daughter Pijana), Trasuns Helena (son Vladislav, daughter Lucija), Trasuns Jazep, Trasuns Stanislav, Trasuns Tereza, Trascenoks Aleksandr, Traks Viktor, Trauberg Karl, Trauberg Maksi, Traucins Janis, Traumanis Imant . . .

The most powerful chemical in the solvent that has for years now been eating away at the fabric of the Soviet Empire, and that will in the end bring it crashing down in ruin, is nationalism; it is no accident and no wonder that of all the dissident groups those most savagely and relentlessly persecuted have been the Ukrainians, for the Ukraine is the largest and most determined of all the captive lands within the Soviet Union's own borders, and the slightest sign of weakness or mercy at the governing centre might set going a fire that could never be put out.

Stalin knew that, which is why he massacred Latvians, Lithuanians and Estonians in such numbers, and his successors have known, and still do know, the same truth. Of course, the knowledge will do them no good; the urge to be free is stronger than all the chains and jails and common graves, all the truncheons of Stalin's NKVD and today's wet-canvas torture in the Soviet Union's madhouses-for-the-sane.

What, will the line stretch out to the crack of doom? Yes, indeed it will. For every entry in *These Names Accuse*, indeed for every victim whose name is now forever lost, there are two more Latvians determined that the cause for which they died – freedom, peace and Latvia – shall one day triumph. I am sure they are right; meanwhile . . .

. . . Zilinskis Vladislav, Zilvinskis Ignats, Zilvinskis Janis, Zins Feodor, Zins Nikolajs, Zins Vladimir, Ziznevkis Vladimir, Ziva Jilijs, Ziznevkaaja Olga, Zmuida Vladislav, Zogots Janis, Zogots Stanislav, Zogots Vladislav, Zoldkovskis Alfons, Zube Herman . . .

The Times   August 8th, 1983

Ghostly don

M. R. James: An Informal Portrait by Michael Cox*

THIS BOOK TELLS me more about M. R. James than I
really wish to know, but its principal drawback is
not the fault of the author, for the truth is that James's
life was exceptionally, perhaps almost uniquely, unin-
teresting, and the main features of it could be accommo-
dated on half a sheet of writing paper, even though Mr
Cox takes a third of the book to bring his subject to the
end of his undergraduate days.

M. R. James was born in 1862; he spent almost every
minute of his life at Eton or King's College, Cambridge
(at both he began *in statu pupillari* and ended as Provost);
he wrote the ghost stories for which alone he is remembered; he was a meticulous scholar, an expert on
medieval manuscripts and the Apocrypha; he was disliked by very few and loved by very many; he died in
1936 and was tidily buried; the rest is silence.

It says much for Mr Cox, then, that his biography of
this spinsterish figure, as insubstantial as many of his
spectres, holds the attention throughout. The reason is
that the author paints with great conviction and success
a picture of a world infinitely remote from that of today

*Oxford, 1983.

173

in character, yet close enough in time to be clearly recognisable. In this world one was brought up in a country parsonage, one naturally went to Eton and subsequently found oneself, by no means to one's surprise, at King's; thereafter, if one was not killed in the First World War (which one probably was), one moved on, in an inevitable progress, to be, say, Master of Trinity, Head of Repton or Bishop of Worcester. (Occasionally, things went wrong, and one – like the horrible Oscar Browning – found it best to go and live in Rome for the rest of one's life. If so, one was mentioned discreetly, if at all, in the memoirs of those who had known one.)

Such a one was 'Monty' James. His biographer's approach to him is pious, even reverential, but I must say that there were times when I disliked him quite a lot. He was forever proclaiming his reluctance to take the jobs that beckoned, and insisting, in the creepiest manner, on his unworthiness for them, but he made sharp use of his elbows when a rival for them appeared; Mr Cox's artlessly revealing account of his hero's election as Provost of King's is something less than edifying, and James hung on to the Directorship of the Fitzwilliam, a post for which he was conspicuously unfitted and which he clearly neglected (his successor, Sir Sydney Cockerell, said bluntly that on taking over he found it 'a pigsty'), far too long.

His attitudes, too, are unappealing; no doubt he was very much of his Victorian time, but so were his contemporaries, and not all of them fought so hard against the admission of women students to Cambridge, or set their faces implacably against science, or called Joyce 'that prostitutor of our language', or went to Salzburg and found it full of churches in 'that particular style which makes me quite ill' (there are a dozen churches in Salzburg wholly or partly by Fischer von Erlach, the greatest master of the Baroque), or so

typified the stupidity of the English refusal to understand Ireland ('They call Parnell the murdered chief, for
some reason best known to themselves'), or censored
the rude bits when translating Walter Map's *De Nugis
Curialium*, or, above all, were so astonishingly inimical
to thought itself.

It is clear that James never had an idea in his life, but
what is much more remarkable is his hostility to ideas in
the young; he was devoted to his charges, at both Eton
and King's, and took infinite trouble to bring them out
and reassure them, but he had nothing in him of the
teacher who delights to encourage intellectual specula-
tion, knowing that it is an essential ingredient in a
mature mind and that if the habit is not acquired early it
is unlikely to be acquired at all.

A. C. Benson, one of James's lifelong friends, is a
much less attractive figure than the invariably cour-
teous, gentle and unmalicious James, but he was
evidently a good judge of character:

> . . . I don't think Monty James is in the palace at all
> – he seems to me to be nothing but a servant in the
> antechamber, handing things to those who go in.
> MRJ has an immense and accurate memory for
> details . . . but not the least constructive or poetical
> power . . . his mind is the mind of a nice child . . . if
> it were not for his humour he would be frozen, dull,
> inaccessible; the very worst kind of don . . . I don't
> suppose anyone alive knows so much or so little
> worth knowing . . . He seems to me an almost per-
> fect instance of high talent; a perfect second-rate man.

Benson even spotted the weakness in the justly
celebrated ghost stories (they are still in print); the
people in them, he said, 'are like elderly dons'. I suppose
the truth is that James was born an elderly don, and was
never really comfortable in any other company.

Yet the affection, gratitude and admiration which he inspired, and for which Mr Cox provides abundant evidence, were obviously real. Here is Mr Jo Grimond, for instance, getting tight, *aetat* thirteen, at the table of the Provost of Eton; it may be said that the milk of human kindness flows so gently in Mr Grimond's veins that he is incapable of a harsh thought, let alone remark, but this is formidable evidence none the less:

> It was his presence and his unspoken encouragement to get others to talk, rather than what he said, that enhanced him . . . the most impressive man I have ever met. It is impossible to compare him with Churchill or de Gaulle, wrapt about in the aura of their achievements. But in force of personality he struck me, perhaps because I was younger when I knew him, and knew him better, as more redoubtable than either.

The ghost stories are James's memorial, and will remain so. They are built up with great skill from innocent beginnings in very ordinary surroundings, until, as James put it himself, 'into this calm environment, let the ominous thing put out its head, unobtrusively at first, and then more insistently, until it holds the stage'. It is this technique that makes the tales so effective, and that to this day can oblige a late-night reader with any imagination, even as he shuts the book muttering that such things are absurd and impossible and a waste of a grown man's time, to look behind the bedroom curtains before switching the light off, just in case.

Observer July 3rd, 1983

The descent of man

L AST WEEK THE Princess of Wales, arriving for a
concert at the Barbican, was faced by a group of
howling demonstrators who, doubtless to her extreme
surprise, screamed 'Murderer!' at her before they were
removed from her path.

You never know, I suppose. Shakespeare said there's
no art to find the mind's construction in the face, and
the received wisdom of the ages has it that still waters
run deep. So it is possible that Her Royal Highness, for
all the innocent charm she displays, becomes after dark a
kind of Jacqueline the Ripper, and by now has the blood
of scores upon her hands. But I do not think it is likely.

Very well; they didn't mean it literally. The ranters
and roarers wanted to show not that the Princess is
exceptionally horrid, hateful and homicidal but that
they are themselves most frightfully compassionate,
caring and concerned. They were demonstrating against
the wearing of fur coats, especially mink ones, because
they hold that it is wrong to kill animals for their fur.
(As it happens, the Princess was not wearing a fur coat
at the time, so unless she goes in for mink knickers the
protest was misplaced anyway. But ranters and roarers
are notoriously no friends to logic.)

The day before, other ranters and roarers (or, much
more likely, the same ones) were demonstrating outside

177

the Savoy, where the Woman of the Year lunch was being held (in aid of a worthy charity, incidentally). The demonstration was directed against Erin Pizzey, whose name will be familiar to most people in connexion with her work in founding and running a refuge for women who had fled (often with their children) from violent husbands. In this instance, the ranters and roarers were not trying to show that wife-battering was an admirable practice; for all I know they may be just as much opposed to it as Mrs Pizzey is. Their complaint was that, in a book she had just published, she has pointed out, as is obviously true, that some women are deeply masochistic and have a psychological need to be treated violently. The ranters and roarers made their point with slogans quite as elegant, thoughtful and perceptive as those which greeted the Princess of Wales; they included 'Erin Pizzey batters women' and 'Pizzey, women's hate of the year'.

There was a most instructive newspaper photograph the day after the demonstration against the Princess of Wales. It showed one of the female fur-howlers, caught in mid-howl, and two things were immediately noticeable about her: first, her face was contorted not with love for animals but with hate for human beings; and second, she was very ugly. That second point, though I shall not dwell on it, is not irrelevant; the Princesse de Lamballe was hacked to pieces by the mob not because she was an aristocrat but because she was much more beautiful than the *tricoteuses*, and they knew it.

As anyone who does not go about with eyes bandaged and ears plugged must know, hardly a week now passes without a demonstration of this kind: that is, a demonstration in which no rational argument is put forward, in which abuse, often obscene, is the only verbal currency employed, in which the professed object of the demonstration is plainly of little or no consequence to the demonstrators, and in which intoler-

178

ance and fanaticism reach truly totalitarian levels.

It is, I think, the intolerance and fanaticism that is especially interesting, and especially important for us to face. Those who howled imprecations at Mrs Pizzey, who has quite certainly done more to help ill-treated women and children than all the ranters and roarers put together, had seized upon the fact that she has now suggested that the problem of violence within the family is not quite so simple as the demonstrators would like it to be. The terror of deviation from an *idée reçue*, which for these people is the greatest terror of all, leads to a desire to blot out the deviation by silencing or even destroying the deviant.

That is what animated the more repulsively bigoted opponents of any easing of the laws against homosexual behaviour; an almost insane terror of discovering that the question of gender is not clear-cut. But it does not have to be a question with such deep psychological roots. A few years ago Miss Jill Tweedie, the *Guardian* columnist, whose radical credentials are impeccable, wrote an article in which she described a visit to a comprehensive school. The article was descriptive only, not polemical; it hardly even came to any conclusions. But in it, because she is an honest reporter, she described things which inevitably implied that that particular school, though comprehensive, left much to be desired. She was abused for weeks in the newspaper's letters column by correspondents for whom the idea that there might be something wrong with a comprehensive school was simply not to be tolerated. But that was an early and a mild example of the phenomenon which I have described, and which has now reached the point at which not even howling and screaming will suffice to express the terror and hatred that possess these fanatics; at the Conservative Party conference last month delegates entering the hall were spat upon by the demonstrators.

This totalitarian intolerance is not the same as, though obviously it overlaps, the more straightforwardly political kind; those who want to turn this country into a Stalinist or Trotskyist dictatorship are no doubt moved by reasons more difficult to elicit and understand than the ones they profess, but the ones they profess are at any rate based on a view consciously held, and an argument rationally deployed. But the ranters and roarers at the Barbican and the Savoy are, in the most chilling sense of that always chilling word, nihilists.

We have been familiar for some time with those whose only intelligible wish for the society they live in is to destroy it. Now we must get to know those who wish to destroy mind itself, and the seat of whose thought processes appears to be not the brain but the tonsils. But the desire to destroy mind wells up from a stream so deep and so dark that it can only be described as anti-life; I sometimes think that if our world is destroyed in a nuclear cataclysm it will be because the hatred of life itself has grown too widespread and too strong to be resisted.

O judgment! thou art fled to brutish beasts, And men have lost their reason! They had better get it back before it is too late. When I was a student of Sir Karl Popper's he once faced us, in a lecture, with a conundrum. Suppose, he said, that you could prove to a Nazi that Nazism was erroneous and wicked – really prove it, so that he was entirely convinced. Would you wish to do so, and would you think it worthwhile? Yes, we said, of course. 'But what', said the sage, 'if the Nazi replies, "I spit on your proof," and shoots you?' We fell silent at the extraordinary paradox of a mind that rejects mind. We would not, I think, find it so extraordinary today.

The Times November 3rd, 1982

180

Sicilian vespers

A Man of Honour: The Autobiography of a Godfather
by Joseph Bonanno*

THIS MENDACIOUS, ILLITERATE and disgusting book is
the life-story of the gangster on whom at least the
film (I have not read the book) of *The Godfather* must
have been based. Bonanno, nicknamed 'Joe Bananas' in
the world of organised crime that he inhabits, comes
from Sicily; both sides of his family were full of
criminals. His father was a thief and a murderer, who
fled to the United States to escape retribution, whether
from the authorities or rival criminals is not clear, but
returned, the danger having passed, when he learned
that others were trying to take over his gang.

He died in the First World War, leaving little Joseph
to be watched over, and trained in crime, by his
Magaddino uncles. When Mussolini came to power,
and made war on the Sicilian gangs who had for so long
preyed on the poorest of the poor, Bonannos and
Magaddinos alike faced a thin future (Joseph, a natural
Fascist if ever there was one, is comically indignant
about Mussolini, who was, after all, interfering in his
family business, even though 'the rustic culture of the

*Deutsch, 1983.

181

island condoned the activities' – that is to say, the peasants were murdered if they didn't meet the extortioners' demands), and our hero fled to America, as his father had done before him, no doubt, thinking that the pickings would be better there.

They were indeed. Chicago was too dangerous for a new criminal entrepreneur, being the exclusive fief of Capone, but New York had plenty to offer; many of his relations were already in business there – business then being mainly extortion, gambling rackets, bootlegging and prostitution. (He claims, with more comic indignation, that he never had anything to do with the last – *ah, monsieur, quelle délicatesse!* – but his kind were always whoremasters.)

He obviously showed promise as a thug, particularly in the internecine war between gangs, and at the remarkably early age of twenty-six was able to take over one of the most powerful of the criminal bands, which he led for many years, alternately making treaties with the other gang-leaders and fighting them as soon as he saw that betrayal – his natural mode – would pay better. The book, indeed, is a roll-call of the scum of the earth; among those with whom Bonanno worked or fought are such familiar names as Luciano, Genovese, Costello, Anastasia, Lucchese and Colombo.

Only one thing distinguishes Bonanno from these otherwise fully interchangeable hoodlums; his incessant whining self-exculpation. He is not content to be a rich criminal (he became very rich indeed before New York got too hot for him as his power slipped away, and he fled to Arizona under the pretence of retiring); he insists on being regarded as a model citizen.

Thus, when he gets a job as bodyguard to a leading murderer, 'I was much like a squire in the service of a knight'; when he gets into the shakedown business. 'What is seen as extortion from the outsider is viewed as self-protection by the insider'; when one gang succeeds in wiping out the leadership of another and celebrates with a banquet at which the guests find it wise to give money to their host, 'It was no different really from when, let's say, the President of the United States is the honoured guest at a $100-a-plate dinner'; when he has been a gang-leader for several years, killing, racketeering, bribing and stealing, 'My name was clean, my reputation solid'; when he thinks about getting this book written, he decides against certain 'would-be biographers' because 'My deepest thoughts, my meditations and my philosophy did not truly interest them.' His greatest indignation, however, is reserved for the police, who finally got him convicted, though only on a charge of conspiring to obstruct the course of justice, just as Capone was found guilty only of tax evasion.

He actually gave himself a heart-attack from rage at the way the FBI was pursuing him, questioning his associates, tapping his telephone and even on one occasion searching his house, on no better grounds than that he is a murderer, extortioner, thief, swindler, racketeer and drug-trafficker:

> The memory of that wanton ransacking of my house is seared in my mind . . . Each time one of these vandals stepped into a closet or pulled out a drawer I felt as if he were violating me.

The book is described as having been written 'with Sergio Lalli'. Who he is is not revealed, but I must say that even if Bonanno does not know one end of a pencil from the other, he would have been well advised to do the job himself; Lalli has obviously heard of something called 'writing', and feels that he ought to shove bits of it in from time to time, the result being passages like 'I was dumbstruck by the perverted whimsy of life' and 'My fastidiousness has been known to drive some people to nervous frustration. Instead of allowing my

183

idiosyncrasies to unnerve her, however, Fay would circumnavigate them.' Much of the book is anyway unreadable, consisting of matter like a Robert Benchley parody:

> He said he had called DiCaro to the office to rebuke him and to humiliate him in front of Scalise. DiCaro's sin was that he talked too much. DiCaro had heard Maranzano express his discontent over Stefano Magaddino. Foolishly DiCaro repeated what he had heard to Gaetano Gagliano . . . Gagliano had told his right-hand man Lucchese, who then brought it back to Maranzano. That's how Maranzano had found out DiCaro had been babbling.

And now? Bonanno is old and ill and frightened, and will die very soon, of disease or a rival's bullet. His two sons are worthless rubbish, petty criminals in and out of jail. His gang is in other hands. His 'respectable' friends, happy to hobnob with him in the days of his ascendancy, no longer return his telephone calls. Nobody will make another sanitised and admiring film about him. He has put his name to a book which shows him to be one of the most swinish human beings who ever lived. I closed it wishing for the first time in my life that I could believe in hell. And also wondering why Mr André Deutsch has seen fit to publish it.

Observer   September 11th, 1983

Commit no nuisance

THERE IS SOMETHING about the words 'Writers' Conference' that makes the heart sink, and my heart duly sank, a week or two ago in New York, when I read a report of a literary gabfest, thus entitled, that was going on there. The theme was 'commitment', and the argument was between those who believe that a writer has a duty to be a political activist in his writing and those who argue the contrary.

The reason the heart sinks at the very thought of writers conferring *en masse* is immediately apparent from the premises of this conference as defined above, in which there are no fewer than *four* giant fallacies. Before turning to them, however, I must mention one very noticeable aspect of the proceedings, which was the apologetic tone taken by those who did not think that writers have a special obligation to be political activists in their work. Typical of this attitude was the view expressed by John Irving, who could not even bring himself to say 'I try to keep out my strongest feelings from my novels' without immediately adding 'but I do spill blood in my books'. Clearly, writers who do not feel like 'political activism' also feel guilty at their lack of what their fellows are telling them is an essential quality of being a writer at all.

It is, however, the fallacies in the assumptions behind

the gathering that interest me most. First, and most urgently, what are writers doing at a 'writers' conference' at all? Apart from the sin of Onan, I cannot think of any human activity that comes so close to the very definition of an inescapably solitary endeavour.

No writing can exist other than that which is conceived in a human mind, and no human mind will conceive and give birth in a manner identical to any other. What, then, can writers have in common, which makes it worth their while to get together and talk about it? The only thing they have in common is that they write; but nothing at all can be deduced about any of them from that fact. All conferences of writers are based on the extraordinarily idiotic notion that writers can have some kind of collective identity issuing in a collective opinion, or – and some of the organisers of such outings would think this a dangerously lax concession – two contrasted collective opinions. But why in the name of Remington, Waterman and Caran d'Ache should writers be expected, only because they are writers, to achieve something that is obviously unachievable by butchers, bakers, candlestick-makers, or men who earn a respectable though inevitably modest living by teaching budgerigars to say 'My name's Joey, what's yours?'

That is not the worst of it. The very idea of asking writers what they think *as writers* has the remarkable effect of simultaneously elevating the writer to an eminence he has done nothing to deserve by merely being a writer, and degrading him by narrowing that which he has in common with his fellow men – his humanity – to the ultimately trivial test of what he does for a living.

Chesterton once came upon a newspaper article which asked, 'Should shop assistants marry?', and had some excellent sport in devising parallel imbecilities, such as 'Is burning good for firewood?' and 'Do feet harm boots?' Those who ask writers to say what writers should collectively think are in the position of the man who wrote the article, and equally unconscious of the fact that they have got things rather upside-down.

Besides, there is the third fallacy: the argument is a tautology. Leaving out consideration of a writer in a totalitarian country who simply writes what he is told to, and who is no more a writer than a fountain pen is, where can a writer's commitment come from? Obviously it can only come from some conviction he holds and wants to express. But then he is an activist by that fact alone and no quantity of writers' conferences demanding activism from each other can affect his position; if he feels committed he is committed, and if he isn't committed he doesn't feel committed, and there is nothing to be conferred about.

Which brings me to the fourth fallacy. Strictly, it cannot be deduced, unlike the other three, from the mere existence of such a conference with such a theme, though anyone familiar with the normal composition of organised gatherings of writers will be able to guess it, and for those who cannot there was useful guidance in New York from a German writer named Fritz Raddatz, who said:

> It is the task of the writer to be not only radical on paper but fighting outside, far beyond what a book can do. If writers could carry out their fantasies and fears, politicians would not dare to do what they do to us. Politicians have no dreams.

The important sentence is the first, though the second and third ought to be preserved beneath a glass dome, like a stuffed pheasant, as an example of the Higher Bosh in its purest form; the only thing politicians 'do to' writers in countries like ours and Herr Raddatz's is to take them far more seriously than they have ever shown

187

any sign of deserving, and to give them a substantial quantity of other people's money to enable them to insult both the politicians and the people more comfortably.

'It is the task of the writer to be not only radical on paper but fighting outside . . . ' Oh, is it indeed? I am not familiar with Herr Raddatz's writing, but sight unseen I am willing to wager that if that is his attitude the only use to which his books could be put by anyone who valued the printed word would be as a support for a billiard-table with one leg shorter than the other three. For his attitude, thus expressed, draws attention to the last of the fallacies in the New York *Syllabus Errorum*, the belief that 'activism' means, and must mean, left-wing activism. 'Radical' is a word that does not in itself imply any political position. But it is invariably used by the kind of people who frequent writers' conferences to mean opposition to the political values of the only countries which give them the freedom to confer.

The most urgent duty of any writer today is to insist, and to go on insisting, that writers have no urgent duties, as writers, to anything but writing. As citizens, taxpayers, parents, car-drivers, dog-owners, householders or members of the Association of Butter Blenders and Butter and Cheese Packers, writers have certain clear and definable duties. They also have the *right*, common to all in free countries, to be politically active in radical causes. But to claim, as does Herr Raddatz (with the obvious approval of many of the others at the conference), that a writer, because he is a writer, *must* be a political activist not only outside his work but inside it also, and moreover that his political activism must be of the 'radical' persuasion, is to run the risk of reminding people like me that not so very long ago there were some frightfully committed writers in Herr Raddatz's country, as politically active as he could wish, and one of them wrote a book called *Mein Kampf*, which called for more political activism than even he might have the stomach for.

Cobblers should stick to their last. What is more, they do. Gardeners garden, publicans pull pints, woodworkers work wood, fishmongers mong fish; and none of these thinks it odd or culpable so to do. Only writers, it seems, gather in covens to lay strange burdens upon one another's backs, burdens which have nothing to do with writing but everything to do with 'activism'.

I am myself a writer of sorts, and few of my regular readers will suppose that I am without strong opinions. But it is not my writing that forms my opinions; it is my opinions that form my writing. The last word on the subject was said by Mary Renault, and I commend her view of the matter not only to Herr Raddatz but to any writer who is tempted to go to a writers' conference and there demand, or agree to the demands of others, that writers should assume a collective identity and propagate a collective cause:

> I have yet to be persuaded that the word 'committed', if analysis is pressed home, will ever be found to mean anything which does not boil down to 'a state in which something else matters more than truth'. There is nothing amusing about committal; the victims of that slaughter lie strewn around.

The Times March 30th, 1983

Out of this world

I LEFT MY annual visit to the cinema dangerously late in 1982, slipping it in only a few days before Christmas. I went to the Empire, Leicester Square, where the film inside might have been designed – indeed, in a larger sense, it plainly was – to induce a spirit so benign and heartening that what we are watching ceases to be entertainment and becomes a truly transformative experience. That, of course, is a definition of art, and anyone who argues that *E. T.* is not a work of art is – well, Shakespeare had a word for him:

> The man that hath no music in himself,
> Nor is not mov'd with concord of sweet sounds,
> Is fit for treasons, stratagems and spoils;
> The motions of his spirit are dull as night,
> And his affections dark as Erebus;
> Let no such man be trusted.

They exist, naturally, as they existed among those who yawned their way through *Nicholas Nickleby*; one such tittering idiot with a singularly misplaced idea of his own superiority has announced that *E. T.* is only a product of an irredeemably debased culture (God send British film-makers, and indeed British culture, such debasing). For *E. T.*, like the RSC's Dickensian

190

triumph, is a test not only of the ability to feel – i.e., to be human – but even more of the willingness to admit feeling – i.e., to express humanity – and more still of the much subtler gift of discrimination among feelings. Of course, at *E.T.* there will be tears in the eyes of anyone who is not actually dead, buried and decomposed; but that is an effect that can be achieved by lesser film-makers with lesser films. Steven Spielberg achieves it by seizing, as did Dickens and his interpreters at the RSC, on the crucial principle at the heart of the universe: *the Manichee is wrong.* Though hate, cruelty, pain and fear abound, love is stronger.

Clad in this impenetrable armour, Spielberg goes forth on his crusade. As anyone who has not spent the past year or so in a sealed igloo will know, *E.T.* is the story of a creature from a far-off star, accidentally stranded on earth, who makes friends with a child; he in turn recruits his baby sister and elder brother into the conspiracy, and then, in the film's colossal, storming finish, adds the circle of children who had earlier expressed only jeering scepticism, and finally draws in his mother to make the *laager* complete.

But why the defensiveness? Why should Elliot feel that he must protect his new friend from the adult world? Because he realises, with the unerring emotional instinct of childhood, that the adults will only want to examine E.T., to use him, to explore him as they would an unfamiliar species of earthly insect. In the world of the scientists to whom E.T. will be handed over if the secret is discovered (it is) there is no room for feeling, and Elliot, who is fortunately too young to have learnt that feeling is dangerous and must be repressed by mind, strives to keep E.T. out of such hands, as the bond between them strengthens. As it happens, Spielberg's insight goes even further, for one of the scientists has retained the child's sense of harmony in the universe, and ends up when E.T. is 'captured', on the side

191

of truth and right: he is rewarded by being present at the final parting, as E.T. prepares to board the spacecraft that has returned in search of him.

Those last minutes are as profoundly affecting as anything I have ever seen in the cinema, a theatre or even an opera-house, and I shall return to them in a moment. But long before they are reached, the audience has been pierced by the effect of this ravishing master-piece and the poetic imagination that informs it throughout. Elliot's first encounter with the still unseen E.T. sets the tone; unable to convince the family that there is *something* at the bottom of the garden, he goes out alone at night to watch. He thinks he hears a sound from the shed, and tosses a ball into it to flush whatever is there; whatever is there, still unseen, tosses it back.

When E.T. is inside the house and Elliot's siblings are in the secret, the next task is to keep the news from mother, through an increasingly hilarious sequence of near-discoveries, the most enchanting of which takes place during her search of Elliot's room, provoked by her realisation that something odd is going on. She throws open the toy-cupboard, and the camera ranges, as her eye does, along the shelf of teddy-bears, lions, frogs and other goggle-eyed stuffed animals, real and fabulous; among them, unblinking and innocent, is the face of the newcomer, and she shuts the cupboard without seeing him.

E.T. has telepathic and other supernatural attributes, including, significantly, the power of healing. But he cannot heal himself, and the scientists and doctors, equipped with every kind of advanced life-saving equipment, watch him fade away, until they are obliged to pronounce life extinct. Elliot slips back into the room; heart-broken at his unique and irreplaceable loss, he utters the password, a word of four letters that is not to be found in any edition of Gray's *Anatomy*, but that nevertheless can, literally, raise the dead incorruptible.

There follows an epic combination of chase and battle; children against adults, bicycle against car, heart against mind, self against ego, faith against technology, yes against no. The children's aim is to get E.T. to his rendezvous with the rescuing ship; the adults' is to stop them, and preserve E.T. for their all too human purposes. And at the moment when the adults have finally got the children, with their precious passenger, cornered, the whole phalanx of bicycles takes off, soaring over the heads of the frustrated pursuers and swooping, in exultation, down to the clearing in the woods, and victory.

There remains only the parting. 'Come,' croaks E.T. 'Stay,' whispers Elliot. But they both know it cannot be. Kid sister steps forward and gives E.T. a brisk, sweet peck on the cheek; big brother puts out a gentle hand and strokes the alien head; then Elliot and E.T. enfold each other in a long, loving embrace. The little creature ascends the ladder, and the space-ship takes off, painting as it goes God's own sign across the heavens, the sign that once told another fearful voyager that all shall be well, and all shall be well, and all manner of thing shall be well.

You could say that *E.T.* is the comic version of *Close Encounters of the Third Kind*. But that describes only the form; the essence of both films is the same, and is of the highest seriousness. It was, indeed, once put in words as serious as any ever heard by mortal ears:

Verily I say unto you, Except ye be converted, and become as little children, ye shall not enter into the kingdom of heaven. Whosoever therefore shall humble himself as this little child, the same is greatest in the kingdom of heaven. And whoso shall receive one such little child in my name receiveth me. But whoso shall offend one of these little ones which believe in me, it were better for him that a millstone were

193

hanged about his neck, and that he were drowned in the depth of the sea.

In that sense, *E.T.* is a film for children, and the magic creature itself a child. But then, in that sense to be a child is the noblest ambition to which we can aspire. It is the mark of Spielberg's achievement that with this film he gives us all the opportunity to attain that ambition. Whether we take it or not is up to us.

The Times   January 22nd, 1983

Nothing extenuate

The Rosenberg File by Ronald Radosh and Joyce Milton*

IN THE HAGIOGRAPHY of the Left, the two principal saints and martyrs of the American Persecution are Julius and Ethel Rosenberg, executed in 1953 for passing secret information to the Soviet Union. (Alger Hiss, convicted only of a non-capital offence, has had to be content with Beatification.) For thirty years, it has been an article of faith, believed in no less passionately by the *bien-pensants* of the West than is the Miracle of St Januarius by Neapolitans, that the Rosenbergs were framed, as the Cold War got into its stride, *pour encourager les autres* (those of them, that is, who had not already been sufficiently *encouragés* by the activities of Senator McCarthy).

The trouble with that argument (apart from the fact that it was obviously untrue) was that it tended to obscure two rather less hysterical, and more important, matters; first, that although the Rosenbergs were guilty, they should still not have been executed, and second, that there were so many defects in the way both the prosecution and the defence were conducted (to say nothing of the behaviour of the trial judge) that on an unprejudiced reading of all the facts they should have had their appeal upheld.

*Weidenfeld and Nicolson, 1983.

195

The trouble with *that* argument is that until the Freedom of Information Act made possible such an unprejudiced reading of all the facts, there was no way in which enough of the truth could be established to convince even those capable of conviction.

This volume, which does indeed establish all the facts, analysing and presenting them with masterly lucidity and grace, is based on a scrupulous and exhaustive study of all the existing evidence (transcripts, secondary sources, historical and political contexts), together with mountains of private files newly made available to the authors, scores of interviews, and no fewer than 200,000 pages of documents released under the Act. It leaves even less room to doubt its conclusions than did Allen Weinstein's similarly massive investigation of the Hiss case, and it will have the same effect – that is, it will make not the slightest difference to those who believe, *alla Napolitana*, that the Rosenbergs were the victims of an anti-semitic, Americo-fascist, warmongering conspiracy of unprecedented evil, presided over by the satanic Eisenhower – ('gnädiger Gauleiter', Ethel called him in one of her letters from the death cell), and resolved upon the murder of two harmless, peace-loving individuals, in order to destroy by terror all possibility of resistance to the conspiracy's plans.

Professor Radosh and Miss Milton are both to be found left of centre on the political spectrum; both grew up in the belief that the Rosenbergs were not guilty; both have been convinced otherwise by the evidence, and by nothing else at all. In their book they marshal that evidence and with it ride down, one by one, the entrenched positions of the believers in the Rosenbergs' innocence.

They demonstrate that both Julius and Ethel were dedicated Soviet-line Communists, that Julius ran a spy-ring and that Ethel was almost certainly his chief accomplice, that the principal witnesses against them,

Herbert Gold and David Greenglass, told the truth
(with the possible exception of one statement of Gold's
that helped to incriminate Ethel – and even that was
probably due to confusion rather than perjury). One by
one, they have tracked down the elusive Snarks of the
Rosenberg mythology; the argument that Greenglass
would not have had enough technical knowledge to
carry out his alleged role; the mystery of the supposedly
forged hotel registration-card that was held to show that
Gold was a hired liar but can now be seen to show
nothing of the kind; even the famous table that was or
was not used for photocopying secret documents, did or
did not cost more than twenty dollars. In years to come,
when this book is read by people with no prior knowledge of, nor interest in, the story it tells, they will
marvel at such rigorous scholarship (the authors even *sic*
obvious transcribing errors), set against a background
of such wisdom and compassion.

But the authors have shown more than all that. They
show – nothing extenuate, nor set down aught in malice
– how the Communist Party first abandoned the Rosenbergs to their fate and then realised that the case could be
used to distract attention from the real frame-up of the
Slansky show-trials in Prague, whereupon they made it
the *cause célèbre* that it has remained ever since for some.
They show how the infighting between the FBI and the
prosecutors was based not on a desire to get at the truth
but on greed for recognition and kudos. They even –
which I would have thought literally impossible – show
that assistant prosecutor Roy Cohn was even more
unspeakable than he showed himself later as Joseph
McCarthy's ball-boy.

They show also how the case represented something
much wider than the matter of the Rosenbergs' crime,
and how it still does:

One well-known left-wing lawyer, for instance,

opened an interview with me by stating bluntly: 'I'm not one of those who think the Rosenbergs weren't engaged in espionage.' Then he went on to threaten to sue if this statement were ever attributed to him and to lecture me on the necessity of presenting the Rosenbergs solely as victims of Cold War hysteria.

Professor Radosh duly leaves him unidentified, but it is not difficult to put a name to him. It is even easier to put a name to his attitude, which is the same as that held by many of Hiss's defenders. The terrible truth is that even if these were convinced – say by open confession – that Hiss and the Rosenbergs had indeed done the things specified in the indictment and had therefore been justly convicted and punished by, respectively, prison and the electric chair, they would not think a whit less of their heroes. (And let us not think that such a failure of the moral imagination is confined to the United States; when Anthony Blunt fell, there were letters in *The Times* which said that the writers admired him no less, and letters in the *Guardian* which went further, and actually commended Blunt for spying on behalf of the Soviet Union.)

America does not come well out of this story. Though the Rosenbergs *were* spies, and were *not* framed, they died (bravely, it must be said) at least partly because of the climate of the times. This book enshrines their pitiful story, and its fairness and honesty provide their only possible memorial.

Observer   October 22nd, 1983

All fall down

ON MARCH 13TH, a skyscraper extension to a luxury hotel in Tokyo is due to be opened. It will be some thirty-odd storeys high, and its appearance will closely match that of the existing block, which is about half the height of the new tower.

The management promises 'wide corridors and comfortable restaurants' (and this in 'a city where space is hard to come by'), an 'expansive mood' and 'traditional luxury'. There are to be 363 guest rooms in the new wing, together with twenty-one suites, seven of them residential, a glass-enclosed swimming-pool, seventy 'top-brand boutiques' and a banquet hall. The 'fashionable Ginza shopping area' is nearby, as is the business and financial centre, to say nothing of 'lovely Hibiya Park – a jogger's delight'.

From photographs of the new premises it seems that the additional block, though not particularly imaginative in design, is inoffensive in appearance and even passably elegant. No doubt it will serve a need, and I have no reason to suppose that the management's claims about the interior and the facilities are at all exaggerated.

Nevertheless, I hope it falls down before it officially opens its doors. What is more, I hope it falls squarely athwart the existing block and reduces that, as well as itself, to rubble. What is more still, I hope that when

disaster strikes the entire Board of Directors are carous-
ing in the banquet hall, eating in the comfortable
restaurants, pacing the wide corridors, swimming in the
glass-enclosed pool, or shopping in the top-brand
boutiques. And finally, and most important of all, I
hope the hotel falls down because of an earthquake.

I speak, as can be seen, with some feeling. For the
hotel in question is the Imperial, and it stands on the site
of one of the greatest crimes ever committed against art
and civilisation; and the criminals were the owners of
the hotel.

Shortly after the outbreak of the First World War,
representatives of a Japanese business consortium commissioned Frank Lloyd Wright, the greatest of all
American architects, and one of the greatest and most
influential the world has ever known in any country
and at any period, to build a hotel in Tokyo which was
to be named, in honour of the ruler of Japan, the Imperial. Wright transferred his principles of 'organic
architecture' to the Orient; the Imperial picked up and
suggested Japanese themes without being in any way a
pastiche or imitation, but it also reflected Wright's
American outlook and fiercely individual style, and the
building in addition had a hint of Mexico and the
Aztecs. Yet for all these mingled themes it was a miracle
of unity and feeling; I stayed there in 1965, and remember vividly the sensation of harmony, naturalness and
peace that the building exuded.

But in Japan, as elsewhere, the voice of money is
louder than that of art. The old Imperial was broad but
low; it covered a vast area but contained, by modern
standards, few rooms. By the time I got there (Wright
died in 1959) a new block had been built beside it,
conforming to the criteria of space and accountancy that
rule the hotel world today.

No matter; the old Imperial still stood, built of
green-tinted lava and bricks the colour of lions, and

sensible visitors like me eschewed the modernity next door, as we eschew the modern tower of the Taj Hotel in Bombay and insist on a room in the old section beside it.

In 1967, however, the voice of money cried more loudly still, and the old Imperial was demolished, to make way for the block that has now been joined by the Imperial Tower. A few voices were raised in the rest of the world against this unspeakable act of barbarism, mine among them; and of course there were others in Japan itself. But nothing would stop Moloch before he had devoured Wright's masterpiece, and in due course the sacrifice was made.

Though my library contains many books by and about Wright, I have seen few of his buildings except in photographs. The Guggenheim Museum in New York, of course; the Morris shop in San Francisco; the Kalita Humphreys Theatre in Dallas; and the Imperial Hotel in Tokyo. The last was the greatest; I have just refreshed my first-hand memories of it by looking at pictures of it and details of its construction.

Which brings me to the new Imperial Tower and my hope that it will be felled by an earthquake. For the syndicate, headed by the redoubtable Baron Okura, who engaged Wright to build the old hotel, made one extra stipulation; it should be able to withstand *les tremblements de terre*. Wright outwitted the irresistible force by virtually floating the hotel on the mud which lay sixty feet below the surface; its supports, he said, in a phrase that has passed into history, would balance the building 'as a waiter's fingers balance a tray'.

His claim was soon to be tested. A year after the building was finished, Tokyo was ravaged by an earthquake. The Imperial rocked but stood, and Okura sent Wright – who had at first been led to believe that his masterpiece had perished – the famous telegram: IMPERIAL STANDS UNDAMAGED AS MONUMENT OF YOUR

GENIUS HUNDREDS OF HOMELESS PROVIDED WITH PER-
FECTLY MAINTAINED SERVICE CONGRATULATIONS.

Whenever I think of the destruction of Wright's
Imperial Hotel, and of my stay there, I am filled with a
great, useless rage at the meanness of spirit displayed by
the Tokyo developers and the blindness and cowardice
of the Japanese authorities who permitted it to be
destroyed, though our own developers and successive
governments, national and municipal, are in no position
to point the finger.

Do you remember, for instance, the uproar over the
proposed demolition of the Nash 'pepperpots' in the
Strand a few years ago, and the cheers that rang out
when it was announced that they were to be saved by an
ingenious compromise? Well, go and look at the absurd
greenhouse that has been stuck in the middle of the
block, while the pepperpots look sadly across it; you
will not need a visit to Tokyo to feel the rage of
desecration. (And the chances of an earthquake de-
molishing Coutts' Bank – it's their greenhouse – with all
its directors are too remote to raise the hopes.) If your
memory is good enough, you can feel the rage even
more strongly by looking into the opening off the
southern side of Cockspur Street, where there used to
be a little, ancient courtyard, a miracle of proportion
and life. I fell in love in that courtyard, more years ago
than I am willing to remember, but no one could fall in
love there now, amid the ugliness that replaced the
harmony when money tore it down.

I know what the answer will be – that we cannot live
in the past or preserve every fragment of it; I would be
more inclined to give up the role of *laudator temporis acti*
if our modern architects were putting up anything of
any distinction. But in any case the destruction of Frank
Lloyd Wright's Imperial Hotel ranks with the destruction of the Temple of Diana by Herostratus, and at least
posterity unanimously curses his name; even I cannot

tell you the name of those who accomplished the modern equivalent in Tokyo, and for all I know the present owners and directors of the new Imperial had nothing at all to do with the murder of the old, and will perish in the ruins, if my curse proves efficacious, as innocent martyrs.

I don't care; we owe God a death, and the fall of the Imperial Tower would be a warning for ever to those who are tempted to destroy what is beautiful to make way for what is only profitable. To our knees, then; and thereafter to our seismographs, where we shall await the answer to our prayers. If the answer is favourable, I suppose it would be presumptuous of us to send a congratulatory telegram, in our turn, to the architect of the earthquake.

The Times   March 5th, 1983

In the sure and certain hope

I HAVE TO set the scene for today's column by first describing a strange experience – particularly strange so soon after my visit to the Soviet propaganda exhibition at the Festival Hall – which was both tragic and exhilarating. I went to the Royal Exchange Theatre in Manchester to see a play which affirms everything the exhibition denies.

Before I turn to my principal theme, then, I must pause to salute it. It is called *Hope Against Hope*, and is adapted by Caspar Wrede (who also directs) mainly from the two volumes of memoirs, published in the West, by Nadezhda, the widow of Osip Mandelstam. Mandelstam was clearly one of the greatest of Russian poets; the play also incorporates a good deal of his poetry, as well as the words of Anna Akhmatova, the Mandelstams' devoted, selfless and beloved friend. (Mandelstam's work would have perished utterly, after his death in one of Stalin's concentration camps, had not Nadezhda – whose very name means 'hope' in Russian – simply learnt it by heart.)

The play is staged with a savage simplicity (even the Royal Exchange's notorious echo is put to devasting use in making more dreadful the sound of death's midnight knock at the door), and acted, particularly by Dilys Hamlett as Akhmatova, in a pure, unadorned style that

204

hammers home the truth and power of its terrible story. For what we see, and indeed share as we watch, is the effect on human beings of the Terror, the most stupendous act of mass murder in the history of the world, in its numbers not equalled even by the Nazis; and its effect was to spread over an entire nation a stifling and pervasive fear, never to be escaped even in sleep, which envelops the characters on Mr Wrede's stage like a cloud of poison gas.

Yet – and this is why we emerge from the theatre not cast down but uplifted – the play also shows that the divine spark in the human spirit can never be extinguished; like the July 20th plotters against Hitler, strangled in nooses of piano wire suspended from meat-hooks, the quality of these people eclipsed the fate they suffered, and built a monument to humanity out of their own bodies. (The play has only three more performances to run – one tonight and two tomorrow – and is worth a long day's journey to Manchester.)

But when *Hope Against Hope* opened three weeks ago, the play was reviewed in the *Guardian* by Robin Thornber, and I must confess that I had no idea that such Stalinoid muck was still being peddled in this country:

> We all know, from careful perusal of the *Reader's Digest*, that the USSR does not enjoy a gentle regime and that it was especially harsh in the 1930s. We are all on the side of the angels and the Jews. Do we really need a propagandist sob story like this? . . . The stage is filled with rugged peasants and grey-uniformed security men as the episodic angst rolls around from Moscow into exile and back. It was a grim life. But was it really? The picture we are painted here is one of an unstable nutter, paranoid from the start, with an exaggerated sense of his own importance. And when he was exiled – rather than executed – to a country town, these appalling snobs

are worried that they are excluded from the twelve
most desirable cities to live among 'wretched people'
and there is nothing for them to do except manual
labour.

Savour that passage, please, Who says that the USSR
'does not enjoy a gentle regime'? Why, the notoriously
right-wing *Reader's Digest*, which would be bound to
decry the achievements of Socialism, would it not? To
be sure, the 1930s were 'especially harsh', but presumably only the *Reader's Digest* and assorted 'appalling
snobs', 'unstable nutters' and sufferers from 'episodic
angst' would seriously argue that an era in which fifteen
million men, women and children were starved, beaten
or frozen to death (the lucky ones were shot) was not
just *especially* harsh but *too* harsh. And those who take a
story of wickedness and nobility, and put it upon a
stage, are engaging in a 'propagandist sob story'. Besides, apart from being frightfully exaggerated by the
Reader's Digest, the whole thing is unnecessary, because
'We are all on the side of the angels and the Jews.' (I
understand that some of Mr Thornber's best friends are
angels.)

Now even if the play *were* propaganda, rather than
the overwhelming experience of truth, art, love and
sacrifice that it is, the passage I have quoted would
surely make Mr Thornber a leading contender in my
competition for human baseness. To portray such
valiant and upright figures as the Mandelstams and
Akhmatova and those brave, free spirits who helped
them at the risk (and in many cases the cost) of their
own lives as effete snobs and liars, half-mad and wholly
unpleasant, is to mock the innocent dead and cry down
goodness. Anyone who has seen the play, or sees it
during the next two days, will know what a squalid
travesty Mr Thornber's account is; a single scene, say
the one in which the Mandelstams are driven from pillar

206

to post, trying to find somewhere – anywhere – to live, will show as much. But to present the few men and women who dared to resist murder as insignificant riff-raff is to make good and evil change places, and if there are too many of Mr Thornber's kind that change will be permanent.

Yet what I have quoted from him is still not the worst. Here is the concluding sentence of his review, his final judgment on Osip Mandelstam: 'It's hardly surprising that his pathetic attempt to sell out with a grovelling "Ode to Stalin" didn't save his skin.'

Mandelstam, while the long-drawn game of arrest and release was going on, was driven, as he was meant to be, to the edge of madness and of suicide. Believing that if he were destroyed his beloved Nadezhda would be killed also, he set himself to try to make his peace with the implacable 'peasant-slayer' (the phrase, in one of his poems, that set his martyrdom in motion). Any fully human being, as Mandelstam comes to the scene in which he struggles with his soul, his mind, his very body, to commit the necessary crime against his art, must ache to stretch out a hand in succour to the writhing man, to say what Nadezhda said after his death:

> While others wrote their odes in their apartments and country villas and were rewarded for them, M wrote his with a rope round his neck. Akhmatova did the same, as they drew the noose tighter round the neck of her son. Who will condemn them for these poems?

Who will condemn them? Why, Mr Thornber will. Mandelstam, after all, faced only torture and death for himself, his wife and his friends, while the heroic Mr Thornber might at any moment catch his finger between two typewriter-keys and sustain a nasty graze;

207

has not such a man the right to jeer at the 'pathetic' Mandelstam's unsuccessful endeavour to 'sell out' by 'grovelling', and to crow at the fact that it didn't 'save his skin'?

No, he hasn't, for to write words like those about a man like that is to dirty and diminish mankind. The Mandelstams' goodness and heroism will live long after Mr Thornber's ashes have been scattered on a dunghill; yet to release such words into the world is an act of darkness in itself, and the darkness is not illuminated by comparisons. Such an article deserves not just condemnation but, in a very real sense, exorcism, and that is why I have today thought it worthwhile to devote such space to the worthless. Mandelstam, and the millions who perished with him, are beyond any more of this world's pain. But we who live have a duty to the past, and one vital part of that duty is to ensure that the graves of the innocents, though forever lost, are tended with reverence.

I salute the memory of Osip Mandelstam, poet, Jew and martyr, and of his virtuous wife, a treasure beyond rubies, whose name was Hope.*

The Times   February 25th 1983

---

* There was an odd sequel to this story. Some months later, Mr Thornber invited me to write a review, for a magazine with which he was connected, of a volume of Mandelstam's poems in translation; his letter, in passing, tried to excuse his behaviour. I replied that I would do the review if I could include in it the whole of this article. I heard no more from him.

Deadlines

Man of Wars: William Howard Russell of 'The Times'
by Alan Hankinson*

THERE IS A tribe of journalists who are never happy
unless other people – preferably hairy, irregularly
dressed and speaking in barbaric tongues – are trying to
kill them. If they are not allowed to go crawling
through jungles infested with flame-throwers and beri-
beri, or to spend their time ducking paving-stones
outside the Presidential Palace when it is being stormed
by the mob, they decline rapidly, and emergency
restorative treatment, such as a couple of weeks in
Beirut or Cambodia, is often necessary if they are not to
perish.

The father of those foreign correspondents whose
chief delight is saying ha-ha among the trumpets is the
subject of this absorbing book. It was Russell's dis-
patches to *The Times* during the Crimean War that
exposed the frightful conditions in which the troops
were living and – in enormous numbers – dying;
indeed, if it had not been for Russell only a handful of
the expeditionary force would have survived, without
most of the dead suffering so much as a scratch from a
Russian bullet or bayonet.

*Heinemann, 1982.

209

That much is well known; but from Mr Hankinson's study – neat, well-marshalled and based on thorough and extensive research – we can now learn that this, the first notable achievement of his career as a journalist, was only the precursor of a series of reports from the front which spanned a quarter of a century and ended in his arriving just too late for the main encounters of the Zulu War.

Russell was Irish born (he spoke with a brogue throughout his life), a heavy drinker and addicted to cards, always in debt, never able to sort out his expenses and constantly losing his luggage (war reporting, evidently, was not the only journalistic tradition he founded). He married at twenty-six, lovingly but tragically, for his wife proved to be unable to manage her strange grass-widow life, and existed to the end in a haze of mental breakdown. Perhaps his difficulties at home made him not unwilling to spend so much time abroad, but there is no doubt that he had something like a vocation for attending upon wars, and would have gone to them wife or no wife.

He had, to a remarkable degree – possibly unique until the generation of correspondents who flourished in the Second World War and the enduring troubles of the post-war world – the gift of the 'nose': that is, of being in the right place at the right moment. Arriving at Königgratz for the decisive battle of the Austro-Prussian War, he climbed to the top of a sixteenth-century tower in the village and had a perfect view of the whole encounter. Covering the Franco-Prussian War he had even greater luck at the crucial engagement:

It was still dark when Russell was wakened with the message 'The Crown Prince has sent to tell you to come to the battle.' At the top of a hill looking across the Meuse to Sedan he found the King, Bismarck and Moltke . . .

But of course that wasn't 'luck' at all. Russell had earned the message from the Crown Prince, the grand-stand overlooking Sedan and the proximity of the commanders, and he had earned these privileges by his unwavering integrity as a journalist as well as his outstanding skill. Everyone, including those who hated him most (they hated him *because* of his integrity), knew that Russell wrote the truth of what he saw, regardless of the feelings of those who read it. This led, from the Crimea onwards, to the crudest abuse and vilification, and at times – for instance in reporting the American Civil War – to real danger; he had a remarkable record of escaping death, sometimes very narrowly indeed, at the hands of those his impartiality had displeased.

From start to finish he had one supreme advantage: Delane, who emerges from this book with still further enhanced stature. The greatest editor *The Times* has had, perhaps the greatest editor this country has ever produced, Delane backed Russell from the first, and continued to do so even when their sympathies parted – *The Times* inclined to the South in 1861, whereas Russell saw more clearly not only that the North *would* win, but that it *should*. And he thought that for the best of all reasons: his profound moral revulsion at the thought of slavery.

It was on a basis of almost faultless moral judgment that Russell built his career; this comes out best in his coverage of the Indian Mutiny, in which he not only attacked, with a bitterness and savagery rare for him, the brutal methods by which it was put down and the atrocities which followed (such as the shooting of unarmed men who had surrendered), but displayed what was for its time, and perhaps for any time, a remarkably understanding and far-sighted attitude to the relations between Britain and India:

I must say that I have been struck with the arrogant

and repellent manner in which we often treat natives of rank, and with the unnecessary harshness of our treatment of inferiors.

. . . There is no association, no intercourse, except of a discreditable kind, between Europeans and natives . . . The habit of speaking of all natives as niggers has recently become quite common . . . it must be remembered that, great as may be the British power in India, it is great only so long as its exercise is consonant with the feelings of the people of India . . . I believe that we can never preserve India by brute force alone except at a cost which will swallow up all the wealth of the home country . . .

Russell earned every particle of the esteem in which he was so widely held, as he earned the friendship of Thackeray and Dickens, the Duke of Sutherland and the Crimean rank-and-file; he earned them by the quality of his character and the attractiveness of his personality. He stands out as a journalist no matter what era he is compared with; he stands out as a human being to the same degree.

Observer December 19th, 1982

De mortuis

THE REVEREND OSCAR MUSPRATT is the Vicar of Penn, and I must say I rather like the cut of his jib. It was to him that, at the end of last week, there fell the task of conducting the funeral service for Donald Maclean, whose parents are buried in Penn churchyard, and whose son had brought back his ashes from Moscow to lie with them in the family grave; the only other mourners were Maclean's brother and sister-in-law.

Because of the delay caused by traffic conditions, darkness had fallen by the time the burial party was assembled, and the service was conducted by the light of torches held by the vicar and the verger:

> We buried him darkly at dead of night,
> The sods with our bayonets turning
> By the struggling moonbeam's misty light
> And the lanthorn dimly burning.

Mr Muspratt was at pains to defend his decision to allow the traitor's remains a resting-place and to conduct the service, saying that he was expecting criticism for doing so. I dare say he will get it, too, though some of it may come from an unexpected quarter; there are folk whose only complaint will be that Mr Muspratt did not read the Funeral Oration of Pericles at the graveside

213

and laud Maclean as a noble hero who did his bit to bring the delights of Soviet Communism to his native country.

Never mind; the good shepherd did his duty by the blackest of his flock, and explained his action in eloquent terms: 'I thought it through', he said, 'and decided what was fair and what was right. I can't say I will bury the goodies and toss out the baddies.'

Lightly they'll talk of the spirit that's gone.
And o'er his cold ashes upbraid him –
But little he'll reck, if they let him sleep on
In the grave where a Briton has laid him.

'A vicar conducting a burial service', went on Mr Muspratt, 'commends everyone to the mercy of God,' and he will no doubt be cheered to know that I commend his sound grasp of theology. It may be said that Maclean escaped earthly punishment for his earthly wickedness (though I for one do not believe he did – beside a quarter of a century of disillusion in Moscow the flames of hell themselves would seem positively inviting, let alone a stretch in Parkhurst) and that he is therefore all the less worthy of Christian burial. But the Book of Common Prayer makes no such distinctions; the office for the burial of the dead says that 'We meekly beseech thee, O Father, to raise us from the death of sin unto the life of righteousness,' and goes on to ask that 'at the general Resurrection in the last day, we may be found acceptable in thy sight.' This is all pretty tentative, and could hardly be otherwise without the most appalling presumption, but the hope there expressed is at the heart of the Christian religion; surely even the greatest sinner may be allowed to hope, and even if he does not, a priest may be allowed at his graveside to hope on his behalf – indeed, that is the very office and function of a priest. Besides, as Mr Muspratt said, 'The dead are dead; one has to serve and minister to the living.'

> We thought, as we hollow'd his narrow bed
> And smooth'd down his lonely pillow,
> That the foe and the stranger would tread o'er his
>   head,
> And we far away on the billow!

It is the modern fashion to affect a lack of interest in the ceremonies that follow death, and even in the mystery of what may follow the ceremonies. So much the worse for the modern fashion, for the mystery remains one of the most tremendous questions in the universe, and the ceremonies, in all ages and cultures except and until our own, have been designed to bring home that tremendousness. The Christian is instructed not to question the purposes of God, which cannot be understood in earthly terms, but the reward for this abstinence is the promise of redemption, which is held out to saint and sinner alike, and neither sainthood nor sinnerdom can be guaranteed to turn the scale in either direction. Heinrich Heine died with one of history's most splendid jests on his lips – *'Dieu me pardonnera, c'est son métier'* – but though Heine was an even odder Christian than he was a Jew, he had got a great truth by the tail.

Donald Maclean committed one of the most terrible of crimes, perhaps the most terrible of all, and let us have no more nonsense about misplaced idealism; he did great evil that greater evil might come. Yesterday I stood beside the grave of Rebecca West, one of the noblest spirits I have ever been fortunate to count as a friend; it was from her, moreover, that I learned exactly why treason, like murder, strikes not only at the state and its citizens but at the very fabric of the universe. She would not have gone to Donald Maclean's funeral, and neither would I, but though the Vicar of Penn would certainly share our earthly view of the traitor and his treason, the clerk had business in the churchyard that the laity had not.

It must be said that the worms take much the same view of these matters as Christianity does, and will munch their way as happily through the remains of the dishonourable son as through those of his honourable parents. It is possible, is it not, that the worms and the Christians have, by different routes and with different motives, both come to the right conclusion? We have it on very good authority that, although five sparrows are sold for two farthings, not one of them is forgotten before God; it is not necessary to see what larger purpose Donald Maclean served, provided we can grasp the strange thought that such purpose might have existed. The sparrows, it is true, did not betray their country, but I doubt if God is quite so literal; I am not a Christian, but I do not find it *very* difficult to believe that there is a category in which, just as there shall be neither Greek nor Jew, circumcision nor uncircumcision, Barbarian, Scythian, bond nor free, so the line between loyal and disloyal shall be likewise erased.

That category is not to be found on earth. But the Vicar of Penn's charity was not of the earthly kind, and anyway we do not even know, you and I and the vicar, what remorse gnawed at Maclean through the solitary years, let alone *in articulo mortis*. If he had returned to Britain and stood trial, he would have been rightly condemned and rightly punished. If another judgment, whether harsher or less harsh than the judgment of men, awaited him in that country churchyard, it was outside our understanding, and the vicar was right to insist, in the absence of clear evidence to the contrary, that it hath pleased Almighty God to take unto himself the soul of our dear brother here departed. To bury a man in consecrated ground is to say nothing about him other

than that God may have a use for his soul, and what
Christian priest could say less? There are still plenty,
after all, to render unto Caesar the things that are
Caesar's:

> Few and short were the prayers we said,
> And we spoke not a word of sorrow;
> But we steadfastly gazed on the face that was dead,
> And we bitterly thought of the morrow.

The Times   March 22nd, 1983

Origins and lemmings

THE OTHER DAY I wrote a column about the tireless efforts being made by some Liberals to ruin their own party. The headline was 'For Liberals read lemmings'.

Whenever a newspaper article figures in legal proceedings – in a libel action, say – somebody has to explain to the judge and the lawyers that writing journalists do not write their own headlines. This is partly for technical reasons with which I shall not burden you, and partly because the art of headline-writing is not at all the same as the art of writing the words underneath; many of the most gifted of newspaper journalists do not have that particular skill at all.

Headlines are written by people called sub-editors, and it was they who wrote the headline I have referred to. The subs, as we call them, are an odd but endearing species; no one who has seen them emerging, at edition time, from nearby burrows (called 'pubs'), blinking at the light and licking the last drops off their whiskers, can fail to warm to the merry creatures, in appearance somewhat resembling koala-bears and really not unlike lemmings themselves. All sensible journalists take care to make friends of the subs; my own relations with them, I am happy to say, are of the most cordial, and not only because I always have a biscuit or two or a

218

knob of sugar in my pockets when I go to see them.

The headline, likening Liberals to lemmings, was inspired, obviously, by the strange habit that lemmings have, well documented through the years, of rushing down to the sea in enormous numbers and drowning themselves. There are two principal theories to explain this curious behaviour. The more romantic is the belief that the lemmings have a deeply rooted biological memory of a sunken continent which, millions of years ago, they inhabited, and that their mass suicides are the fruits of a desperate attempt to find again their lost home or perish in the attempt.

This well-supported and strongly held belief was enshrined in verse by a former poet laureate, John Masefield:

Once in a hundred years the Lemmings come
Westward, in search of food, over the snow;
Westward, until the salt sea drowns them dumb;
Westward, till all are drowned, those Lemmings go.
Once, it is thought, there was a westward land
(Now drowned) where there was food for those
    starved things,
And memory of the place has burnt its brand
In the little brains of all the Lemming kings . . .

The less haunting but more widely held theory for the lemmings' periodic mass suicides, one which fits better into our gloomy times, is that they do it deliberately, out of an excess of *Weltschmerz*, and it is this explanation that has made the lemming so popular a metaphor for those who wish to point to heedless self-destructive urges among humankind; there must by now be several hundred thousand printed references to the 'lemming-like' behaviour of the nuclear powers in their arms race.

Masefield touches upon the second version, too, and

its human analogue, for the rest of the poem I have quoted runs as follows:

> Perhaps, long since, there was a land beyond
> Westward from death, some city, some calm place
> Where one could taste God's quiet and be fond
> With the little beauty of a human face;
> But now the land is drowned. Yet still we press
> Westward, in search, to death, to nothingness.

Now scientists will have none of these theories; lemmings drown themselves in huge numbers, but the experts, though they cannot explain the phenomenon, reject both the belief that the lemmings behave thus in search of Atlantis and the conjecture that they do so to fill *Daily Telegraph* leading articles. Another Poet Laureate, Robert Bridges, was of this more hard-headed school, saying in *The Testament of Beauty* (I am sorry about his horrible orthography) that:

> Ther is no tradition among the lemmings of Norway
> how their progenitors, when their offspring
>   increased,
> bravely forsook their crowded nestes in the snow,
> swarming upon the plains to ravage field and farm,
> and in unswerving course ate their way to the coast,
> where plunging down the rocks they swam in the salt
>   sea
> to drowning death; nor hav they in acting thus today
> any plan for their journey or prospect in the event.

All the foregoing sets out simply the reasons for the place the lemming holds in the imagination of millions who have never set eyes on one of them; whence the headline on my column. What now follows should not be read by those with a history of heart trouble, for the shock to the nervous system that my readers are about to experience might well prove too much for the particularly susceptible.

Lemmings don't. They don't, that is, rush down to the sea and drown themselves, whether in search of a sunken land, or because they have run out of Nembutal, or for any other reason. They do take part in gigantic migrationary movements, and there is evidence that these follow a cyclical pattern – not once a century, as Masefield says, but probably every four years; the reason for these mass uprootings is still not clear, though it seems to have something to do with population pressure. In the course of the migrations, with hordes of lemmings simultaneously on the march, some inevitably get drowned in streams and fjords, and when they reach the coasts many drown in the attempt to reach offshore islands. But the Gadarene Lemming is a mythical animal, and the real one – *Lemmus lemmus* – is entitled to complain about many decades of defamation.

The greatest scholar of lemming-lore is Dr Charles Elton, sometime director of the Bureau of Animal Population in Oxford; his book on the subject, *Voles, Mice and Lemmings* (OUP, 1942), which disposes of many lemming myths, including the one which holds that they are rained from the clouds, is still the standard work on the subject, though there is an excellent, more popular work by Walter Marsden, called *The Lemming Year* (Chatto, 1964) and of course no serious student of the subject can ignore Wildhagen's *Om vekslingene i bestandan av smagnagere i Norge.*

All leading authorities, however, and all field studies, are adamant that the verdict of *felo de se* is, and always has been, a miscarriage of justice; Elton says that 'When a lemming cannot avoid meeting a man he will often sit on his hind legs and hop up and down as if in excited anger and charge the intruder, who may get his hand bitten deeply if he tries to pick the animal up,' and it seems very likely that the lemming's anger and aggressive behaviour have been excited by the tenacious but unjust belief in its suicidal tendencies.

Though the lemming has figured in folklore for a good many centuries, the mass drowning belief is, interestingly enough, a twentieth-century creation. It is, I suppose, a sophisticate's myth, appealing in its deliberate-suicide aspect to fashionable modern pessimism and in its Atlantis-search form to the equally fashionable yearning for a new, pure world elsewhere. Professor Bergen Evans, in that most entertaining work *The Natural History of Nonsense* (Michael Joseph, 1947), points out that it is a popular belief with the *New Yorker*, but the role of lemming mythopoeist to the gentry must long since have been taken over by the *New York Review of Books*.

I do not suppose that my words today will kill the lemming legend; I have often pointed out in vain that Canute did not suppose he could make the waves turn back (he commanded them to do so in order to show up his courtiers, who insisted that he had such powers, for the fools they were), and I have also fruitlessly explained that Cloud-cuckoo-land, invariably used as an insult, is in fact a high compliment, for in Aristophanes' play *The Birds*, Nephelococcugia, or Cloud-cuckoo-land, the kingdom established by the birds midway between heaven and earth, triumphantly brings both gods and men to subjection. Myths, however, have their own power – they would not be myths if they did not – and I do not expect the suicidal lemming to vanish from the earth after today. Still, it might vanish from a few newspaper headlines; and with even that much of an achievement I would be well content.

The Times September 6th, 1983

Murder most fashionable

A *Daily Express* gossip-columnist the other day quoted some remarks made by Claus von Bulow, the Danish-born American who was convicted earlier this year of trying to murder his wife by injecting her with powerful doses of insulin. (She did not die, but lapsed into a coma, apparently irreversible; at any rate she has not regained consciousness after more than six months.) Von Bulow, who is out on bail pending appeal, continues to protest his innocence, and we should remember that that is something done by innocent men as well as guilty ones; in any case, I have nothing to say about the outcome of the trial, let alone of the appeal.

What I *have* something to say about is his claim that most of his friends and many strangers have offered him sympathetic encouragement. He puts forward this information to strengthen his insistence that he is innocent, and in the course of doing so makes the statement that caught my imagination. 'The crime I am said to have committed', he says, 'was unspeakable, and if people believed I had done it they would not treat me in this way.'

Unfortunately – for us rather than him – the apparently logical conclusion is based on a false premise: our world is littered with people who would not think it at all odd to stop a man in the street and offer him their support (which is what von Bulow says is constantly happening to him) though they thought him guilty of an unspeakable attempt at murder.

Not long before the von Bulow case there was the matter of Jack Henry Abbott, who was made almost as famous and popular by Norman Mailer as the murderers of *In Cold Blood* had been by Truman Capote. Abbott was – is – a murderer who began to write to Mr Mailer from prison; he is clearly a man who knows a sucker when he sees one. His letters describe horrible conditions and treatment in the prisons he has been in; some of it, even much of it, may well be true, though confidence in his veracity is not strengthened (except, no doubt, in the mind of Mr Mailer) by passages like this:

> The judge sentenced me to the main penitentiary for the express purpose of having me raped by prisoners and reduced to a homosexual . . . To the authorities, there is nothing seriously wrong with anyone getting raped in prison. On the contrary, the idea excites them; they *enjoy* it.

Anyway, Mr Mailer got together a group of like-minded savants, and with a long pull, a strong pull and a pull all together they managed to obtain parole for Abbott, an event celebrated by a fashionable dinner-party *chez* Mailer. Unfortunately, the guest of honour, pausing only to put his letters to his benefactor into a handy volume (published in this country by Hutchinson) and to knock off an article or two for the *New York Review of Books*, promptly committed another murder – of, it is worth noting, an unprovoked and particularly brutal kind – and was returned to the hoosegow, leaving Mr Mailer in a state of pained bewilderment and the victim of Mr Mailer's friend in a state of rapidly advancing decomposition.

Let us not take a too elevated cisatlantic view of these events. The Kray twins graced many a modish London gathering in their murderous heyday, and when Charles Richardson wrote his famous letter to *The Times* I am sure that the people who concluded from it that he was a much misunderstood man greatly outnumbered those who felt that he had provided the best reason yet devised for abolishing the Open University.

Nor should we forget George Davis; he didn't murder anybody, but about a quarter of an hour after getting out of prison as a result of a campaign in this country similar to the Abbott boom in the United States (you can still see 'George Davis is innocent' painted on walls in London) he was tastelessly photographed by some brash *paparazzo* (apparently indifferent to the Press Council's severe condemnation of 'snatched' pictures) in the very act of holding up a bank with a sawn-off shotgun.

There is a phrase – I think it is Alexander Woollcott's – about 'a girlish enthusiasm for mere biceps', and there is something of that at work here. Not long ago it was fashionable for the daughters of the peerage to form liaisons on the far side of Aldgate Pump with some of the more cauliflower-eared practitioners of gbh, and the excitement generated by the combination of violence and armpits that attracted the Hon. Sophonisba was not entirely confined to her own sex (quite apart from the homosexual *demi-monde* that overlapped with the world of the Krays).

But the deliciously guilty thrill that some obtain from contemplating, at a safe distance, a criminal brutality is inadequate to explain those who want to shake the hand of Claus von Bulow, not because they think he is innocent but because they think he is guilty, or those who clinked glasses with Jack Henry Abbott and so thoroughly encouraged him to dwell in his fantasies that

they were subsequently obliged to feel quite mortified
when he went a little too far, or those who indignantly
agreed with Charles Richardson when he argued that it
was society's fault, not his, that he was a ruthless and
sadistic gangster.

Once upon a time, it was smart to wear certain
clothes, to eat at certain restaurants, to take holidays at
certain expensive resorts. Now palates having grown
jaded, smartness comes in sharper flavours; it is smart to
sniff cocaine, to watch pornographic videotapes, to
despise the clumsy processes of democratic government, above all to affect a moral relativism that puts a
murderer's qualities as an entertaining dinner-guest
above his qualities as a murderer.

For this new smart set life is either literature or a series
of sociological experiments, and is in any case without
responsibility; when there is no one to answer to, there
is nothing to answer. Claus von Bulow may or may not
have tried to murder his wife in a particularly vile
manner, and in doing so reduced her existence to that of
a vegetable, but the parties he gave before this misfor-
tune fell upon him were among Newport's finest, so let
us cross the road and shake his hand. Jack Henry Abbott
may have stuck a knife into a waiter whose manner had
displeased him, and then twisted the knife round in his
dying body, but Mr Norman Mailer, who 'can afford
the sophisticated despair of finding Russia altogether as
abominable as America', says that Abbott may be 'a
new writer of the largest stature', and there are few
judges of new writers, or for that matter of the size of
statures, to compare with Mr Mailer. Charles Richardson may have watched, laughing, as his victims suffered, but anyone can see that that was the fault of the
social *mores* of his *milieu*. If you will forgive me for
quoting myself, I shall repeat what I wrote at the time of
the Blunt affair. 'There are those who live by an ener-
vated reason that owns no master in the soul, and who

can find arguments that enable them to claim that the atrophy of the moral sense from which they suffer is in fact a form of rational judgment.'

The trouble with people who hobnob with fashionable murderers – and indeed choose which murderers are to *be* fashionable and then make them so – is that if they were asked not *whether* it is wrong to do murder, but *why* it is wrong, they would be unable to say, and for the most part would quite literally be unable to see any meaning at all in the question. But if we do not know why murder is wrong then we are as dead as the victim of the least fashionable murderer; even Raskolnikov, in the end, came to know the answer.

It is possible to believe that Claus von Bulow was wrongly convicted. But if you do not believe that, it is impossible for you to shake his hand in merry friendship and save your soul alive. You say you haven't got a soul to save? I rest my case.

The Times   November 15th, 1982

Beyond the fringe

IT IS A truth not sufficiently appreciated that any political proposal which commends itself to both front benches of the House of Commons is at best uscless and at worst against the public interest; one which also appeals to both main parties' back benches is likely to be a constitutional outrage and certain to be seriously damaging to the people's liberty, prosperity or both.

Such is the proposed Representation of the People Bill, of which it can be safely said that the matter of improving the people's representation never so much as entered the heads of the Conservative and Labour politicians who took part in the discussions that led to the Government's White Paper, their sole concern being to reinforce and extend their monopoly of power, or, to put it in plain English, to get more of their bread into more of our gravy; it's God's mercy that they didn't include a provision to double their own salaries and link their pensions to an automatic annual increase of four times the rate of inflation, and they will probably try to shove that bit in on the Report stage if we don't watch out, or even if we do.

In case there is any monoglot Kalmuck newly arrived among us this morning who does not understand what I am talking about, I had better make clear that it is not the extension of the franchise to those on holiday; what makes me think more kindly of Guy Fawkes, Oliver Cromwell and the German pilot who scored a direct hit on the House of Commons during the Blitz is the proposed intention to raise the electoral deposit to a thousand pounds. (The original plan had been to make it *two* thousand pounds, but they magnanimously changed their minds in the course of the discussions.)

The arguments with which this shameful measure has been supported are impudent even beyond the calls of self-interest. First, it is said that when the deposit was instituted (in 1918) the value of money was much greater, so that in equivalent terms £150 should today, be even more than £1,000. Oh yes? And what pray, was the standard percentage of income-tax at that time? And what were average rates? And where was VAT? And how many more of the imposts, multings, duties, levies, tariffs, licences, exactions, fees, dues, tolls, assessments, excises, *gabelles* and capitations now laid upon our backs then existed? And how many small parties or unmoneyed Independents were interested in contesting elections then? And when is the cost of a dog-licence going to be raised, in line with the rate of inflation, for the first time since *it* was instituted, in 1878? (When dog-owners cease to have votes, that's when.)

Second, it is claimed that the cost to the state of a candidature at a parliamentary election is much higher than £150, so that candidates with no hope of election are being subsidised. So they are; so are the candidates *with* hope of election, and they are quite determined to keep things that way, for the only substantial state-paid election cost that can be attributed to individual candidates is the free mailing to all voters, which every candidate is entitled to claim, and this does not in practice benefit 'fringe' candidates at all, since very few of them can afford the printing of the leaflets which the free postal service would distribute, and even fewer have the manpower to address and fill the envelopes. In other words, the argument against subsidising candidates does not apply to the new proposal's victims, but it does apply to the instigators; the cost of the free mailing for the Conservative and Labour parties in a general election (reckoning it as second-class post) is roughly £10 million.

Next, it is contended that the proliferation of eccentric candidates tends to bring the election process into disrepute, a charge which, when I first read it, had the unprecedented effect of rendering me incapable of speech for nearly half an hour; beside the Hattersleys and Healeys, the Proctors and Dickenses, Screaming Lord Sutch was a model of dignity and political uprightness, and a bloody sight funnier into the bargain.

But all that is only by way of refutation of the false claims made on behalf of the new Bill. Much more important is the fact that it will damage democracy, which is no doubt why the Home Office is in favour of it, the attitude of the present Home Secretary to democracy being the same as that of a Victorian maiden aunt to masturbation – he has no idea what it is and would not dream of asking, but is convinced that it makes you go blind. Cannot the two main parties lift their eyes for a moment over the rim of the trough and see how important to the vigour and health of our political life is a constant ebb and flow of people and groups who refuse allegiance to the established parties, and how essential it is that such people and groups shall have *full* access to the political system in all its forms, most particularly in its electoral aspect?

If we are going to deny to the Communist Party and the National Front, the SWP and Vanessa's Loonies, the Ecology Party and Commander Bill Boaks, the genuine (as opposed to purely theoretical) right to put up as full a slate of candidates as they wish and can afford, and if we are going to go even further and deny that right to all but a rich handful of the brave and splendid men and women who stand as genuine Independents, unattached even to the smallest and weirdest of the political *groupuscules*, then we might as well deny them free speech as well, together with the right to publish their views and to solicit support for them. (I wouldn't be in the least surprised to learn that a discussion paper enshrining just such proposals is circulating in the Home Office at this very moment.)

If economic monopolies, whether of capital or labour, are inimical to economic advance, how much more are political monopolies to political progress! Just imagine a political Britain in which the Conservative and Labour parties have their way and extinguish altogether every rival variety of political appeal, starting with the Alliance, against whom, of course, this measure is chiefly directed. Both parties are at present ossified and bureaucratic to an extent which renders them largely indistinguishable from whichever prehistoric monster it was that took twenty minutes to register with its brain the fact that a rival had bitten its tail off; give them another inch of exclusive political rights and they will take another dozen miles of arrogance, chicanery and selfishness.

No doubt the Labour Party will assert that it is not responsible for a government Bill, and – since the contents of it were decided by a Select Committee, not a Speaker's Conference – they are not committed to it. They may even, to keep up a show, attack the clause which gives an absentee vote to those British citizens living abroad. It will all be wool-pulling; this measure is the fruit of a corrupt bargain between Conservatives and Labour, and I do not think the adjective is too strong. All the main provisions of the Bill were agreed by the Select Committee; the fact is that in return for Labour support over the holiday franchise (believed by psephologists to favour the Tories) the Government has offered the lowering of the deposit-losing share of the vote from one-eighth to one-twentieth, thus sparing the Labour Party such hideous and damaging humiliations as their 119 lost deposits of 1983, for under the proposed new rule they would have lost fewer than a dozen. (It is, I may add, particularly dishonest of Labour to sell itself in this fashion, for the original deposit was brought in to limit the chances of the nascent Labour Party, as the present change is designed to hinder the Alliance.)

When this matter was discussed, last week, on Sir Robin Day's *Question Time*, before a studio audience, Dr Rhodes Boyson, for the Tories, put forward the argument that the Bill was to be commended because it would discourage 'extremist parties'. It is a measure of the political vanity which grips the two main parties that even a normally merry and realistic fellow like Dr Boyson can thus render himself incapable of noticing that an extremist party, while it remains within the law, has as much right to propagate its doctrines as he has. And that 'incapable of noticing' is the literal truth; so imbued are both main parties with the belief that they are entitled to *all* the political power and patronage and pelf that our system offers them, which is no little, that they have no idea how monstrous, and how dangerous, is their determination to change the law to ensure that not even the smallest challenge to their monopoly may be mounted except on crippling financial terms.

It is worth recording the fact that when Sir Robin put the question to the audience, a great majority – at least two to one – were against the proposal. But implacably opposed as the established politicians are to sharing power with their less official rivals, they are a hundred times more adamant that they will never share it with the people.

The Times   February 7th, 1984

Monty Verdi to the rescue

CALIBAN LIVES. I deduce this from the goings-on at the Royal Festival Hall and its two adjacent concert-rooms, the Queen Elizabeth Hall and Purcell Room; all three are owned by the GLC, as the heirs of the LCC which built them, and not long ago the rulers of the GLC sacked the manager, and took over the direct running of the halls themselves.

One of the earliest fruits of the change was the scandal of the Soviet propaganda exhibition staged there (at a peppercorn rent); when the details were being worked out, the GLC did not even insist on being allowed to stage a reciprocal exhibition in Moscow, so eager were they to let Londoners know that the Soviet Union is a peace-loving democracy, brimming over with freedom, prosperity and scrupulous concern for the neighbours. (Mind you, a GLC-sponsored exhibition about us would probably have depicted little but accounts of the oppressed wage-slaves in today's Britain and of their struggle to obtain the vote and the right to form trade unions, with huge oil-paintings by Mr Michael Meacher of the said wage-slaves being batoned by police wearing swastika armbands.)

Ever since, the GLC has been resisting, by evasion and delay, any attempt to let Londoners see the other side of the argument, and even now, when they have at last made a half-hearted apology for the Soviet show, they have made it clear that they will not permit any serious or general criticism of the Soviet Union on premises under their control; their only concession is to allow a group working on behalf of Jews who wish to leave the Soviet Union to participate in an Amnesty International exhibition.

At the same time, the new rule at the RFH has brought some substantial improvements – the very attractive liveliness that the foyers now display, largely owing to the outstanding service provided in the buffets by the new caterers, and the improved box office arrangements. (There are the usual rubbishy 'souvenirs' on sale, of course, but even these are more than set off by the excellent bookshop.)

All the same, whatever happens in the surroundings of a concert-hall, good or bad or both, it will and must be judged by what happens inside it. So far, nothing very different has taken place; the GLC have put on various performances and exhibitions in furtherance of their political beliefs (though none, of course, furthering contrary views), but the music remains much the same. As far as I know, there have been no suggestions that bookings will be more readily accepted if the programmes contain more of the works of Alan Bush or loyal contemporary Soviet composers, nor has anybody hinted that putting on performances by Rostropovich, Ashkenazy and other defectors from their glorious Soviet fatherland will be looked on askance. I think I detect a slight tendency to dilute the contents of programmes with a higher proportion of very familiar works, but that, if it is happening, could well be defended (if, indeed, it needs to be defended at all) as sensible commercial practice by the promoters.

Now, however, Caliban has emerged from his lair, blinking at the light and mumbling his watchword: elitist. Mr Peter Pitt, chairthing of the GLC committee under whose auspices the South Bank halls are run, has determined that 'We want more working class and black audiences.' It is a laudable desire, and he is not the first to feel it; the Workers' Educational Association and many similar organisations were conceived in the same spirit. But there is one great, and terrible, difference between the pioneers of art for the masses and the present attitude of the GLC. The former wanted – it was, in many cases, the mainspring of their existence – to illumine the lives of the poor, the uneducated, the despairing, by making sure that they had cheap access to the best that art and craft had created throughout the ages. The wiser among these pioneers knew that those who availed themselves of what was offered would always be a minority, as indeed they have always been a minority among the rich, the educated and the confident; but the pioneers, from William Morris to Arnold Wesker, as they laboured in this field, have always preferred to light candles rather than curse the darkness.

But they never wanted to burn people with the candles. Mr Pitt says 'I don't think many people from my constituency of Hounslow go to the South Bank.' If not, it is a pity, but it is a pity because the musical glories to be found on the South Bank – at, incidentally, ludicrously low prices (£2.80 for the *Missa Solemnis* under Haitink, £1.50 for Ida Haendel playing the Beethoven Violin Concerto, £2.30 for Bach's *St John Passion*) – would enrich the lives of the people of Hounslow, or even the life of Mr Pitt, just as much as they enrich me.

Mr Pitt is not willing to go out and persuade his constituents to try a spot of Chopin, Mozart and other long-haired intellectuals. No, his approach can be understood from the following statement of his credo: 'There are class and race institutionalised barriers here that need to be broken.' Before a claim as mad and pitiful as that (what West Indian, what labourer, has ever been refused service at the RFH Box Office, or sneered at by the white toffs in the next seat?), Beethoven himself would have been tempted to erase the bit about *Seid umschlungen, Millionen* in the Ninth Symphony. But Mr Pitt's intention, which might well have struck Goering as a bit extreme, is now clear. If the masses will not go to art, so much the worse for art. *Delenda est Carthago.*

Therefore, it is announced, we are to have wrestling and snooker at the Festival Hall; parallel delights are being devised for the QEH and the Purcell Room. When the four principal symphony orchestras were asked to think of ways to increase South Bank audiences, the management of the Royal Philharmonic suggested bussing in factory workers, and the LPO proposed to add the Festival Hall to the Albert Hall as a venue for its industrial concerts. But such plans were rejected, and soon the grunts and groans of the judo-artists will mingle with the click of the balls on the green baize, in place of the sounds that South Bank audiences since 1951 and indeed audiences all over the world for half a thousand years, have been used to.

Well, well, we must move with the times. But we need not move with them before expressing our opinion of them. The contempt of the far left for the people whose interests they claim to have at heart is notorious. At election-time the workers have been 'brainwashed by the media'; at public libraries they cannot be trusted to reject distasteful attitudes, so books containing these must be censored off the shelves; in their trade unions they might vote the wrong way if they had secret ballots for their officials, so they must not be allowed to have such ballots; in the Festival Hall foyer they might form views unfavourable to the Soviet Union if such views are on offer there, so offer them access to favourable ones only; and upstairs in the auditorium let them be content with the pig-swill that is all they deserve or are capable of enjoying.

Surely this must be the only era in history, other than that of Nazi Germany, in which excellence is not something to admire and strive for, to encourage and to share, but something to hate and mock, to root out and destroy. In education, the whole thrust of the left is to pull down anything that might set standards for emulation. In housing, the local authority that insists that all front doors must be the same colour is driven by the same hunger for uniformity among the masses. In politics, the growing intolerance on the left – displayed in the hounding out of Labour MPs who will not toe the new line and the shouting down of any opposing voice at meetings – has reached epidemic proportions. And in art, anything that has provided for human beings, and can still provide, a literally infinite breadth and depth of beauty, passion, enlightenment, understanding, inspiration and balm is 'elitist', and must be rejected.

Caliban lives indeed; and he was always averse to seeing his face in the mirror. But now he has people to smash the mirror for him, and the seven years' bad luck that breaking a mirror entails will be borne by the rest of us. And paid for by us, too; the Festival Hall interior will have to be practically rebuilt for an evening of wrestling or snooker, all at prodigious cost. But Caliban now has unlimited access to our money, and unlimited willingness to spend it for his own dark ends. Art on the South Bank, it seems, may have to go into exile, like the government of a nation subjugated by tyranny, until the GLC is swept away and the free republic of true civilisation restored.

The Times February 22nd, 1984

Of tops

WE ARE TOLD on exceptionally good authority that all they that take the sword shall perish with the sword. What is less well known is that all they that take the publicity shall likewise be brought low by the very instrument they have sought to conquer with. The tale which illustrates this truth is one peculiarly of our time; indeed, it could not have taken place in any earlier era. And the moral is not necessarily obvious.

A year or so ago, a young lady among the spectators at a televised rugby international at Twickenham decided, on a sudden impulse, to remove her upper garments and reveal to the cameras and the viewing public that which, or more precisely those which, lay beneath.

What the butler saw, next moment, was an exceptionally substantial bosom, surmounted by an attractive smile. No doubt some of the staider followers of the game (the game of rugby, that is), to whom the turf of Twickers is holy ground, fell down dead at the sight, but for the rest of us (the less expensive Sunday newspapers, next day, featured the lady's development at roughly life-size) the episode served to brighten a chilly weekend, to be pronounced harmless – I forget whether whitehousian moralists declared at the time that the total collapse of civilisation was now inevitable

238

– and to be quickly forgotten.

It was not, however, to be forgotten quite so quickly by the protagonist of the drama, nor was the course of her life destined to continue in quite so pleasant and light-hearted a manner. It seems that today she is without employment, overdrawn at her bank, heavily in debt to the Inland Revenue, pregnant but unmarried, and living, for want of means, in a friend's house, where she shares a room with her younger sister.

If there were any who denounced the bosom-baring as the kind of thing the Declining Romans got up to in their more imaginative moments, they are no doubt now pursing their lips in great satisfaction and concluding that the wages of sin, if not going as far as death, certainly include insolvency, unmarried motherhood and the condemnation of all right-thinking persons. Take your jumper off at Twickenham and the wrath of God is inevitable; if she'd taken her knickers off as well she would certainly have been struck by lightning ere now.

That is not my view, of course. If it was Providence that punished the lady in that fashion, Providence must have a singularly nasty mind. (Particularly, I may say, since the lady seems to have an exceptionally nice one; she has just said that she feels no resentment for the father of her child, that although he is not himself married 'it would not be right to name him', and that she will not be asking him for money.) But what interests me, and provides my real theme, is not the lady's original action, nor her present misfortunes, but the bit in between.

The immediate consequence of her action was her launching, on a sea of *réclame*, into a many-sided new life (she had been, until the fateful day, an assistant in a bookshop). She made a pop record; she opened a boutique; offers of modelling engagements fell thick and fast upon her doormat.

Note carefully the constituent elements of her new triple career, its nature almost incredibly representative of the froth and bubble that this age mistakes for substance. The characteristic sound of our time and place is the howling and gibbering of pop singers; its characteristic product is the shoddy of the King's Road and Carnaby Street; its characteristic activity is posing, with expressionless faces, for the cameras of advertising photographers. The innocent young lady at Twickenham had noticed, as had the rest of us, these phenomena, and had noticed, again like others, that many of those engaged in such trades had become successful and rich – some of them, indeed, rich almost beyond imagining. Why should she not believe the agents and promoters, the spivs and *tummlers*, who told her that she was no less gifted than the successful ones (which was probably true), and could therefore become no less rich?

You can conjugate it as an irregular verb: I am a pop-singer, you own a boutique, she models, we are successful and rich. Why indeed should not the Lady of Twickenham believe that there is a crock of gold at the end of the rainbow, when in our society a bishop scurries across the country to sit at the feet of Mr Mick Jagger and nod sagely at the pearls of wisdom that fall from his ample lips?

'Everyone seems to think,' she says in recounting her disillusionment, 'that because I'm famous I must be rich.' That ought to be carved on the twentieth century's tombstone, not because the lady has so painfully spotted the fallacy, but because she has so artlessly, yet so truly, defined what today is fame. It is to make records so undemanding of emotion, thought or music that they will get into the 'charts'; it is to sell 'designer jeans' and 'costume jewellery' (if there is any more room on the tombstone those phrases ought to be added); it is to narrow the eyes and point one hip and find the resultant picture amid the glossy trash of the latest giveaway property magazine; for that matter, it is to find the proprietor of the latest giveaway property magazine appointed Rector of the Royal College of Art.

As it chanced, the lady in this case failed to become rich. The boutique did not find favour, the record did not sell millions of copies, the modelling offers did not continue; she now, presumably, knows what song the sirens sang. But it might so easily have been otherwise. In our era, some have become millionaires by putting rubbishy records on gramophones; others have made even greater fortunes by gyrating to the records in 'discotheques'; attractive young women have ensured themselves a place in the history books, or at any rate Madame Tussaud's, by looking half-daft for hours on end in a photographic studio. Who will dare say that the young lady of Twickenham was barred from such glories by lack of talent?

And where was the lesson taught that was thus dearly learnt? Who told the disc jockeys and the boutique-owners and the gossip columnists and the disco-dancers and the models that at the end of the rainbow there was gold to be got for the stooping? Why, those who, in the older arts, cottoned on much earlier to the fact that imagination, hard work and the stuff of creation were no longer necessary for success. Do you curl your lip at those who seek fame and fortune through the dubious portals of publicity? Then be prepared to encompass a good deal more in your curl.

For we live in a world that is not exclusively composed of froth; there is the sour lees beneath it to be considered. You can pile bricks for £4,000 a pile if you are in favour at the Tate Gallery; if you tear up the pages of an Act of Parliament and stick them on a wall you may find yourself commended by Mr Richard Cork; if you cover 54 square feet of canvas with rubbish Mr Norman Rosenthal will hang it in the Royal Academy,

and if you cover 500 square feet with even greater
rubbish Mr Christos Joachimides will hang it in the very
next room. Meanwhile, if you are a composer, or want
to be thought one, you may write 'works in which the
voice has no fixed relation to the score', 'works whose
performance is indeterminate' and 'works based on
imperfections in the manuscript paper', and Herr H. H.
Stuckenschmidt will write an admiring book about you.
Alternatively, you can write poetry by cutting words of
newspapers and pasting them together at random; the
editors of literary magazines will be eager to publish the
results and will squeal like stuck pigs if the Arts Council
will not pay them to do so.

It seems hard on the young lady at the rugger match,
who did nothing more wicked than believe what she
had been told about the value of publicity, that she
should now be in want while others, no more talented
than she, should have waxed rich as accidentally as she
has now waxed poor. Their fame, of course, will last,
by history's reckoning, only an instant longer than hers,
and she did, after all, cheer us all up, which is more than
most of them can say; would the Sunday papers bother
to print pictures of Stockhausen's chest, or Carl
André's, or Snoo Wilson's?

Good luck, say I, to the lady with the torso that *did*
provide pictures, who seems to be a brave lass as well as
a good-hearted one; 'I may be down', she says, 'but I'm
not out.' I wonder, however, whether she feels that she
might have done better to stay at her job in the
bookshop and keep all her clothes on. She says herself
that she did not earn more than £8,000 from first to last
after her moment of fame, and is now £7,000 in debt.
But if she were still behind the counter selling the works
of Tolstoy, Sophocles and Levin, I calculate that she
would have made some £5,400. And what is more, had
she remained in the bookshop she might, when trade
was slack, have taken down the appropriate volume of

Of tops

Shakespeare and read these words by way of warning:

All that glisters is not gold;
Often have you heard that told;
Many a man his life hath sold
But my outside to behold;
Gilded tombs do worms infold.
Had you been as wise as bold,
Young in limbs, in judgment old,
Your answer had not been inscroll'd;
Fare you well; your suit is cold.

The Times   March 20th, 1984

Of bottoms

TODAY WE HAVE naming of parts. A week ago, a nobly-born lady, no less than the sister of the Marquess of Dufferin, and not only of Dufferin but of Ava to boot, was mortally insulted at Greenham Common, where she had gone in order to write an article about the nuclear ladies. The nature of the insult is such that I have hesitated long before deciding to give it wider currency, and readers of a respectable disposition would be well advised to consider very carefully whether they would not do better to stop reading this column immediately; in any case I have to give formal notice that neither I nor the Editor of *The Times* can accept any responsibility for any ill-effects suffered by those who stay with me to what I am obliged to call, with dreadful appositeness in the circumstances I am about to relate, the bitter end.

Lady Caroline Hamilton-Temple-Blackwood, to name but a few, has revealed that in the course of her visit a busload of airmen turned their backs, pulled down their trousers and displayed their buttocks to her, with intent to offend. She has described the scene with a vividness that bodes well for her future article about the Greenham protestors, and I cannot do better than repeat her very words. 'They were bending over like ostriches,' she said; 'I had a girl assistant with me and we

244

were both shocked and appalled. I have never seen something so unpleasant.'

I dare say; no wonder she is, according to one report, 'writing to the commander of the camp to demand an explanation', and according to another, 'consulting lawyers with a view to bringing a complaint'. (If she does decide to take legal action, I can warmly recommend a barrister with much experience of this kind of thing, Sir Exemplary Chutzpah, QC.)

Edmund Burke had a word for it:

I saw her just above the horizon, decorating and cheering the elevated sphere she just began to move in, glittering like the morning star, full of life, and splendour, and joy. Little did I dream that I should have lived to see disasters fallen upon her in a nation of gallant men, in a nation of men of honour, and of cavaliers. I thought ten thousand swords must have leaped from their scabbards to avenge even a look that threatened her with insult. But the age of chivalry is gone.

It is indeed; now it is buttocks that leap, not swords, and trousers, not scabbards, that they leap from. And the men's action is no less disgraceful merely because they were apparently under the impression that Lady Caroline was there to demonstrate against nuclear missiles, for apart from anything else, if they will show their buttocks to a lady of title what might they not reveal to the more humbly born? As Lady Caroline said, 'I sympathise with any woman who has to put up with anything like this, regardless of her political allegiance.' And to make matters still worse – if anything *could* be worse than what I have described – the Thames Valley police, when questioned about the matter, said that they knew nothing about it, and added that 'the whole affair should be taken with a pinch of salt'.

At this point, as those who know me will readily suppose, I sent for my horsewhip and looked up the trains to Greenham. What? Insult a nobleman's sister, scion of a marquessate whose origins are lost in the mists of unimaginable antiquity (it goes back to 1888), a shy and tender maiden cloistered until now amid the echoing halls of Clandeboye, the even tenor of her days disturbed by nothing more sensational than a discussion of farm prices over afternoon tea with the McGillicuddy of the Reeks? Do this, and hope to escape a thrashing at the hands of the Chevalier Levin? Perish the thought!

But while I was waiting for the taxi to take me to the station, I read on, and the subtle worm of doubt began to gnaw at the foundations of my anger. In the first place, Lady Caroline added one piece of information that would surely have been better left unadded: 'I don't know if they were Americans', she said, 'because I only saw their buttocks.' (If they had been Russians, of course, they would have had snow on their bottoms.) But it was what followed that caused me to wonder just what I would be getting into if I took action to avenge this stain upon a lady's honour.

For it seems that Lady Caroline, so far from being, as I had assumed, a chit of seventeen who would blush scarlet at the name of Edgar Allan Poe, is a fifty-one-year-old novelist (she writes as Caroline Blackwood) who has been married no fewer than three times, and more to the point (in view of her unwillingness to assign a nationality to the offending buttocks), two of her husbands were American and one British. Not to put too fine a point on it, Lady Caroline has been around.

Her first troth (Marr. diss.) was plighted to Mr Lucian Freud, the painter. Her second hubby (Marr. diss.) was Israel Citkowitz, an American composer. *En troisièmes noces*, she was spliced to Robert Lowell, the poet, who left her a widow in 1977. Now it is no doubt possible that each of these distinguished men invariably wore long woollen combinations while taking a bath, and came to bed clad in a suit of armour. But the hypothesis is sufficiently improbable to be ignored. To speak plainly, I think she has seen a male buttock or two in her time, up to a maximum of six (reckoning two to a husband).

True, a matrimonial buttock bared in the course of domesticity is a far cry from a busload of strangers' buttocks bared to make a political comment; moreover, and irrespective of the intention behind the Greenham buttocks, one can have too much even of a good thing – a chocolate with my coffee is always welcome, but a couple of dozen would tend to cloy, and it may be that what bittermints are to me buttocks are to Lady Caroline. All the same, I have a horrible feeling that I am about to recite the whole of a limerick that begins 'There was a young man of Australia, Who painted his bum as a dahlia . . .' (What is more, in view of the somewhat anatomical paintings of ladies in her first husband's *oeuvre*, she is lucky not to find a more than lifesize portrait of her *pudendum* hanging in the Tate.)

You see, I am sure, what I am driving at. If not, I can make it clear by asking a question. Lady Caroline says that she was 'shocked and appalled'. And my question is: *Was* she? I mean *really*? Really and actually shocked and appalled? Honest? See this wet, see this dry, cross my heart and hope to die? Not just shocked or just appalled but *both*? Furthermore, Lady Caroline says she has 'never seen something so unpleasant'. Never? *Never?* After all, we have established with reasonable certainty that she must have known what a buttock looks like. We also know, because she tells us as much, that she 'only saw their buttocks', which rules out the possibility that in the course of the proceedings the offending airmen turned round. (Mind you, even if they had . . .) Yet she has never seen something so unpleasant.

Au fond, if I may so express myself, it all comes back to my grandmother's celebrated dictum: if you never have anything worse than that to worry about, you won't have done too badly. If Lady Caroline never has greater reason to be shocked and appalled, if she never sees something more unpleasant, than the sight of a row of men's buttocks, she can count herself lucky indeed. The world is full of wars and the rumours of wars; famine, pestilence and sudden death are not yet eradicated; the heart of man still contains ample store of envy, hatred, malice and all uncharitableness. Here, milady, is a leper; over there, an orphaned child weeps; anon comes a procession of beggars, their tin cups empty as their stomachs; that thwack you hear is a tyrant's truncheon on an innocent head.

Still shocked, still appalled, still never seen something so unpleasant? Go to, you great ninny; next time a platoon of airmen, or for that matter an entire regiment of soldiers, show their bottoms to you, try laughing, and if you cannot laugh, turn your head away, and be about your business. Otherwise, I warn you, I shall tell yet again, with a wealth of expression and many a meaningful glance, the story of the old woman who calls a policeman to her home and bids him arrest the man in the house opposite for gross indecency, explaining that the neighbour in question is standing stark naked in a brightly lit and uncurtained window. The policeman peers out, but says he can see no such sight. 'Of course not,' snaps the crone, 'you have to stand on a chair.'

The Times   March 24th, 1984

Living by his wits

A Cup of News: The Life of Thomas Nashe
by Charles Nicholl*

EVERY AGE HAS its literary underworld, just round the corner from Grub Street, where live those truly talented writers who cannot find (or keep) a patron, who drink the advance and sell an entirely different book to an entirely different publisher, who find quarrel in a straw and usually choose those who can harm them to quarrel with. Some of them will turn their hands to anything that can be done with a pen, not excluding pornography, begging letters, forgery, plagiarism and blackmail. Mock them not; they include Chatterton, Corvo, Aretino, Villon himself.

And Thomas Nashe, of whom we have here at last a substantial and scholarly biography. The Elizabethan literary swamp was the most fetid of all; in it there splashed strange beasts – poets and playwrights and pamphleteers who doubled as spies for the Government or the Government's enemies, men who would one day join a plot against the Queen and the next day betray it, secret Papists and noisy Puritans, alchemists and necromancers, Raleigh factions and Leicester factions.

*Routledge & Kegan Paul, 1984.

249

In this seething stew of literature, politics, diabolism, printing and religion bobbed Nashe, who has the honour of being the author of the very first printed reference to Shakespeare. He was one of the 'University Wits'; he lived not more than thirty-four years; he wrote plays (one of them, a joint work with Ben Jonson, was suppressed as slanderous and seditious, and Nashe had to go into hiding while Jonson went to gaol), pamphlets, invective, polemic, the earliest narrative poem about a dildo, the first picaresque novel. He was almost always broke and frequently drunk; he had a giant fit of remorse in mid-career, and wrote a half-mad religious tract in consequence; his last, strangest and finest work was a disquisition in praise of the red herring, a most fitting apotheosis.

Nashe is best known for his part in the 'Martin Marprelate' controversy. This was the pseudonym of a shifting collective of Puritans, publishing their tracts in *samizdat*; their chief target was episcopacy. For Martin, an Anglican Bishop was little better than the Pope; Whitgift, the Archbishop of Canterbury, was 'John of Cant' and 'the pope of Lambehithe'. Whitgift had the idea of casting out Satan with Beelzebub; he enlisted Nashe, among others, to write counter-Martinist tracts and pamphlets, using all Martin's own devices of wit, satire and scurrility.

Such work was right up Nashe's alley, and he did it with such gusto that he frightened his patron into suppressing his later offerings, a perfect instance of Nashe's damaging his prospects by his inability to let well alone. Mr Nicholl suggests that Nashe was a secret Catholic sympathiser, and offers some suggestive titbits to back up his claim. Unfortunately, he then rapidly succumbs to an almost fatal attack of the Spotted Hotsons, in which delirium he can and does make any phrase, however innocuous, pregnant with hidden meanings and allusions ('Once the signal is noticed the whole concealed message becomes clear'); when the fit is most strongly upon him, his 'discoveries' are hardly to be distinguished from the ravings of the Baconians (he even offers a ludicrously feeble cypher for the identification of Holofernes with Florio).

Most scholars agree that Nashe is portrayed by Shakespeare as Moth in *Love's Labour's Lost*, and Mr Nicholl does not dissent from the prevailing view, though I must say I am tempted to see him in Yorick, for he was certainly capable of pouring a flagon of Rhenish on anybody's head. But what has been hitherto neglected, and even by Mr Nicholl is not treated as fully as it might be, is Nashe's extraordinary use of language, which brings to mind Rabelais and Rabelais's translator Urquhart, together with some of the most extreme apocalyptic writing of the two and seventy jarring sects which sprang up in the wake of the Civil War, and indeed even some modern surrealists. Here, for instance, are some of the names he invented to abuse his great enemy, Gabriel Harvey: Gaffer Jobbernoule, Gamaliel Hobgoblin, Gilgilis Hobberdehoy, Gregory Habberdine, Gabriel Hangtelow, Timothy Tiptoes, Braggadochio Glorioso, Infractissime Pistlepragmos, Gibralter, Galpogas and Gabrielissime. And here – it has to be quoted at length if it is to have its effect – is Nashe's terrible and terrified vision of the evil that boiled about him:

> What do we talke of one divel? There is not a room in anie mans house but is pestred and close packed with a campe royall of divels . . . No place (bee it no bigger than a pockhole in a mans face) but is close thronged with them. Infinite millions of them wil hang swarming about a worm-eaten nose. Don Lucifer himselfe, their grand Capitano, asketh no better throne than a bleare eye to set up his state in. Upon a haire they will sit like a nit, and over-dredge a bald

pate like a white scurffe . . . In Westminster Hall a man can scarce breath for them, for in every corner they hover as thick as moates in the sunne. The Druides that dwelt in the Isle of Man, which are famous for great conjurers, are reported to have been lousie with familiars. Had they but put their finger and their thumbe into their neck, they could have pluckt out a whole neast of them.

The obvious question is: is there really enough of Nashe for him to deserve a biography of his own rather than a chapter in someone else's? It is true that Mr Nicholl is sometimes hard pressed. He offers, for instance, fourteen pages of close textual and thematic analysis of a play, *The Isle of Dogs*, of which not a single line apart from the title has survived in print or manuscript, and of which nothing at all is known; a considerable achievement. But there is remarkably little padding elsewhere, nor much need of it; Nashe comes alive in Mr Nicholl's hands, and in doing so demands to be taken seriously; even the author's penchant for seeing things that are not there does not get in the way. Nashe did have genius, warped though it was, and his best work will survive, undamaged by his scribbled worst. And he made friends; he even kept some, one of whom wrote a fitting epitaph:

His stile was wittie, though it had some gall,
Some thing he might have mended, so may all.
Yet this I say, that for a mother witt,
Fewe men have ever seene the like of it.

Observer   March 25th, 1984

Sinister rituals

W HAT WOULD YOU think if you learnt that the
Labour group on Lewisham council had formally
declared that membership of the Labour Party was
incompatible with being a Jew, and that they were now
considering an extension of this doctrine, to the effect
that no Jew could be a member of the council staff, so
that it would follow from such a rule (for Lewisham
council is Labour-controlled) that Jewish employees
would be dismissed? Before you consider that question,
add this one to it (they can probably be answered
together): how would you feel if you were told on good
authority that in Islington, applicants for jobs on the
council's staff are to be required to reveal whether they
are Jews?

Hang on a minute: I want to extend the questionnaire.
Suppose you picked up the *Guardian* and in it read an
item which consisted of nothing but a list of prominent
British citizens who, the writer was claiming to reveal,
were Jews, with the implication that they concealed the
fact: what would your attitude be to that? And what
would it be if you read such an item in that newspaper
on several days in succession, with a fresh register each
day of undercover Jews?

I could go on like this for some time. Well, I *will*.
Describe your feelings on learning that someone had

253

written a book demonstrating (to the author's satisfaction at least) that the Jack the Ripper murders had been committed by a group of men directed by a Jew, the purpose being to hush up a royal scandal which the victims had learnt about, that the mutilations to the women's bodies were in the form of the Jewish Star of David, and that there had been a Jewish conspiracy at the highest level to conceal the Jewish guilt for the crimes. Then, if you will be so kind, consider carefully what would be the nature of your response if you read a more recent book by the same author, sub-titled *The Secret World of the Jews*, in which the writer reveals that he had written to the Lord Chief Justice, the Master of the Rolls, the President of the Family Division of the High Court and the Vice-Chancellor of the Chancery Division of the same, demanding to know whether they were or were not Jews, and clearly felt it very significant, even sinister, that three of them threw his letter into the wastepaper basket and that the reply of the fourth was 'I do not really feel that the question of whether or not I am a Jew is a matter of public concern.'

And finally, just before I reveal what all this is about, tell me what you would think if you read through the whole of the 'Are you a Jew, judge?' book and found it to be composed largely of anonymous tittle-tattle about the hidden but enormous and widespread influence of the Jews in British life eked out by a substantial amount of the kind of stuff otherwise found only in the letters of those who write to me in green ink to reveal that the Archbishop of Canterbury is putting thought-rays into their heads from outer space, and to insist that I should stop him forthwith.

Very well, then; get another cup of coffee and make yourself comfortable. Then, with a red pencil for ease of reference, strike through every mention of Jews in what you have just read, and substitute, as the sense requires, 'Mason', 'Masons', 'Masonic', etc. And *now* tell me what you feel when I say that, when thus – and only thus – amended, every single word I have written is the literal truth. In Lewisham and Islington such steps *have* been taken against Masons; such daily lists of alleged Masons *did* appear in the *Guardian*; there *is* such a book about the Masonic nature of Jack the Ripper's crimes, Masonic mutilations and all (the book is sub-titled, with almost unbelievable insensitivity, *The Final Solution*); the same author, Mr Stephen Knight, *has* just written such a successor, called in full *The Brotherhood: The Secret World of the Freemasons*, in which he reveals that he *did* write to the four senior judges of England, demanding to be told whether they were Masons, and *does* make clear that he thinks their failure to comply a matter for suspicion.

As David Hume would point out even if I do not, it does not logically follow that because one group of people are innocent of the vile charges brought collectively against them another must be equally blameless; I cannot prove that there is no sinister international body working to take over the world with the aid of a plan called *The Protocols of the Elders of Freemasonry*. But it is worth remarking that the nature of many of the charges against Freemasons is astonishingly similar to that of many accusations made against Jews by anti-semites, and that the most virulent of Jew-baiters have commonly been Mason-haters as well. And anyway, what is the difference between a threat to sack Masons just because they are Masons and a threat to sack Jews just because they are Jews?

The point about charges of collective guilt is that they can never be disproved; if a particular Freemason can show beyond any doubt that he has never exerted, or been the beneficiary of, improper Masonic influence or behaviour, the reply of the people like Mr Stephen Knight will always be: of course not, it's the *other* Masons I am talking about. And since there must be bad

255

men who are Masons, as there are bad men who are Jews, and some Masons who help fellow-Masons to preferment or gain, as there are some Jews who do such things for fellow-Jews (and some supporters of Tottenham Hotspur for *their* chums, and some cat-lovers likewise, and some farmers, and some Rastafarians, and some Roman Catholics – ooh, I could tell you a thing or two about what Roman Catholics get up to with their sinister rituals like 'Communion' and 'Confession' and 'Mass' – and some Glaswegians, and some nuclear disarmers, and for that matter some writers of rubbishy books), it will always be possible, on the principle of *crimine ab uno, disce omnes*, to make a number of individuals who have one, and only one, thing in common look like a single many-headed entity whose common element, because it is wrongly used by some of them, is itself and of its very nature to be condemned.

When this practice is directed against Jews, it is called anti-semitism. When it is directed against black people, it is called racism. When it is directed against the uneducated, it is called class prejudice. When it is directed against strange old women, it is called witchhunting. But when it is directed against Freemasons, it is apparently all quite right and proper, at any rate in the eyes of those responsible for the diary of the *Guardian*, in the eyes of those who write books to show that the Jack the Ripper murders were the product of a Masonic conspiracy and follow these up with books which suggest that practically *everything* is the product of a Masonic conspiracy, and in the eyes of those who control the councils of Lewisham and Islington together with, if this evil thing is not crushed now, many another council up and down the land.

I do not suppose that Mr Knight's books and the *Guardian* diary are written with intent to cause harm; nor would I be in favour of censorship of them even if I did. But they are harbingers of a foul spring. And when it comes to the interrogation in Lewisham and Islington of council members and employees as to their Masonic affiliations, no doubt conducted by specially appointed Mason-sniffers like the Jew-sniffers of yesteryear, followed by threats of expulsion or dismissal for those who give off the telltale sulphurous stink, then – why then, I think, it is time for us to take down from the wall the weapons which we fondly believed could be left to gather rust forever, and lay about us with a will, going into battle beneath a banner embroidered with Santayana's words: Those who cannot remember the past are condemned to repeat it.

The Times March 27th, 1984

Index

259

Index

Index

261

Index

Index

Index

Index

265

Index

Index